50 Ancient Roman Cuisine Recipes for Home

By: Kelly Johnson

Table of Contents

- Roast Wild Boar: Season boar with herbs and roast over open fire.
- Stuffed Dormice: Fill dormice with minced pork, herbs, and spices, then roast.
- Stuffed Squid: Fill squid with a mixture of cheese, herbs, and breadcrumbs, then bake.
- Garum: Fermented fish sauce used as a condiment in various dishes.
- Libum: Roman cheesecake made with flour, cheese, eggs, and honey.
- Moretum: Cheese spread with garlic, herbs, and olive oil.
- Isicia Omentata: Spiced beef or pork patties grilled or fried.
- Patina: Savory baked dishes made with eggs, meat, and vegetables.
- Gustum: Appetizers served before the main course.
- Ova Spongia ex Lacte: Egg custard with milk and honey.
- Mellaria: Honey-based desserts and sweets.
- Laganum: Thin flatbread often served with cheese and honey.
- Pullum Numidicum: Chicken cooked with spices and apricots.
- Conditurae: Various sauces and relishes used to flavor dishes.
- Fungi: Mushrooms used in various dishes.
- Gustum de Praecoquis: Dessert made with stewed quinces and honey.
- Pernae: Ham dishes prepared in different ways.
- Conditum Paradoxum: Spiced wine used as a drink or in cooking.
- In Mitulis: Mussels cooked with herbs and wine.
- Gustum de Castaneis: Sweet chestnut dessert.
- Minutal Matianum: Stew made with pork, chicken, or fish.
- Caponata: Eggplant-based dish with vinegar and other vegetables.
- Laganophila: Lamb or pork dishes wrapped in dough and baked.
- Patella: Omelette or quiche-like dish with various ingredients.
- Gustum de Cerebellis: Dessert made with spelt and honey.
- Vitella: Veal dishes cooked in different styles.
- Jowles of Sturgeon: Sturgeon cheeks cooked with herbs and spices.
- Epityrum: Olive relish with herbs and vinegar.
- Frisi Apiciani: Fried fish or seafood.
- Fritillus: Fried pastries served with honey or sweet sauces.
- Aliter Dulcia: Assorted sweet dishes and desserts.
- Alicam: Barley or wheat porridge served with honey.
- Mulsum: Honey-sweetened wine or mead.

- Laserpitium: Aromatic herb used in cooking.
- Cibarium: General term for food or meals.
- Gustum de Pineis: Pine nut desserts and dishes.
- Alicam Cerebellatum: Spelt porridge sweetened with honey.
- Gustum de Persicis: Peach-based desserts.
- Tyropatinam: Cheesecake-like desserts.
- Gustum de Piris: Pear-based dishes and desserts.
- Pisum: Pea dishes prepared with various ingredients.
- Patina Apiciana: Baked dishes named after Apicius.
- Gustum de Nuce: Walnut-based dishes and desserts.
- Panis: Bread, a staple of Roman cuisine.
- Lenticulae: Lentil dishes prepared in different styles.
- Isicium de Lepore: Rabbit or hare dishes prepared with spices.
- Cochleae: Snails cooked with various seasonings.
- Gustum de Pomis: Apple-based dishes and desserts.

Roast Wild Boar: Season boar with herbs and roast over open fire.

Ingredients:

- Wild boar
- Assorted herbs (such as rosemary, thyme, sage)
- Salt
- Olive oil (optional)

Instructions:

1. Prepare the Boar: Clean and prepare the wild boar for roasting. Ensure it is properly dressed and cleaned.
2. Seasoning: Rub the boar generously with salt and coat it with a mixture of chopped herbs. Traditional Roman herbs like rosemary, thyme, and sage work well.
3. Roasting: Place the seasoned boar on a spit or rack over an open fire. Make sure the fire is hot enough to cook the meat evenly.
4. Cooking Time: Roast the boar slowly, turning it regularly to ensure even cooking. Cooking time will vary depending on the size of the boar, but it can take several hours for larger cuts.
5. Basting (Optional): If desired, baste the boar with olive oil or its own juices while cooking to keep it moist and add flavor.
6. Checking Doneness: Use a meat thermometer to check the internal temperature. The boar is done when it reaches an internal temperature of at least 145°F (63°C) for safety.
7. Resting: Once cooked, let the boar rest for a few minutes before carving. This allows the juices to redistribute and ensures a moist and tender roast.
8. Serving: Carve the boar into slices and serve with accompanying sides like roasted vegetables, bread, or sauces.

Roasting wild boar was a favorite method of cooking in ancient Rome and was often reserved for special occasions or feasts. The combination of wild game and aromatic herbs would have made this dish a flavorful centerpiece for any Roman meal.

Stuffed Dormice: Fill dormice with minced pork, herbs, and spices, then roast.

Ingredients:

- Dormice (or substitute small game birds like quail)
- Minced pork (or other ground meat)
- Assorted herbs (such as parsley, mint, and oregano)
- Spices (such as black pepper, cumin, or coriander)
- Salt
- Olive oil (for basting)

Instructions:

1. Prepare the Dormice: Ensure the dormice are properly cleaned and gutted. Alternatively, use small game birds like quail as a substitute.
2. Make the Stuffing: In a bowl, mix together the minced pork with finely chopped herbs and spices. Use a generous amount of herbs to flavor the stuffing mixture.
3. Seasoning: Season the dormice (or birds) with salt, both inside and out.
4. Stuffing: Carefully stuff the dormice with the prepared mixture of minced pork and herbs. Pack the stuffing firmly into the cavity of each dormouse.
5. Securing: If needed, secure the openings of the dormice with toothpicks or kitchen twine to keep the stuffing inside during roasting.
6. Roasting: Place the stuffed dormice on a roasting rack or spit. Roast them in an oven or over an open fire, turning occasionally for even cooking.
7. Basting (Optional): During roasting, baste the dormice with olive oil or their own juices to keep them moist and add flavor.
8. Cooking Time: Roast the dormice until they are fully cooked and the stuffing is hot and cooked through. Cooking time will vary depending on the size of the dormice or birds used.
9. Resting: Once cooked, allow the stuffed dormice to rest for a few minutes before serving. This allows the flavors to meld together.
10. Serving: Serve the stuffed dormice as a unique and flavorful dish, accompanied by Roman-inspired sides like bread, olives, or vegetables.

Stuffed dormice were considered a delicacy in ancient Roman cuisine, often enjoyed at banquets and feasts. The combination of savory minced pork, fragrant herbs, and tender dormice would have created a rich and memorable dish for special occasions.

Stuffed Squid: Fill squid with a mixture of cheese, herbs, and breadcrumbs, then bake.

Ingredients:

- Fresh squid tubes (cleaned and prepared)
- Cheese (such as ricotta, feta, or Parmesan)
- Fresh herbs (such as parsley, basil, or oregano)
- Breadcrumbs
- Olive oil
- Salt and pepper
- Optional: Lemon wedges for serving

Instructions:

1. Prepare the Squid: Ensure the squid tubes are cleaned thoroughly. Remove any membranes and rinse them under cold water. Pat dry with paper towels.
2. Preheat the Oven: Preheat your oven to a moderate temperature, around 375°F (190°C).
3. Make the Stuffing: In a bowl, combine the cheese (crumbled or grated), finely chopped fresh herbs, breadcrumbs, salt, and pepper. Adjust the seasoning to taste.
4. Stuff the Squid: Carefully stuff each squid tube with the prepared cheese and herb mixture. Use a spoon to gently fill the squid tubes, being careful not to overfill.
5. Secure the Squid: Close the openings of the squid tubes with toothpicks or by folding the edges over and securing with skewers, ensuring the stuffing stays inside during baking.
6. Arrange in a Baking Dish: Place the stuffed squid tubes in a lightly greased baking dish, making sure they are in a single layer and not overcrowded.
7. Drizzle with Olive Oil: Drizzle some olive oil over the stuffed squid tubes to help them brown and crisp up during baking.
8. Bake: Transfer the baking dish to the preheated oven and bake for about 20-25 minutes, or until the squid is cooked through and the stuffing is golden and crispy on top.
9. Serve: Remove the stuffed squid from the oven and let them cool slightly. Carefully remove the toothpicks or skewers before serving. Optionally, garnish with lemon wedges for squeezing over the squid.
10. Enjoy: Serve the stuffed squid as a delicious appetizer or main course, accompanied by a salad or other Mediterranean-inspired sides.

This recipe showcases the use of simple ingredients like cheese, herbs, and breadcrumbs to create a flavorful and satisfying dish using fresh squid. It's a delightful example of ancient Roman cuisine, where seafood was often combined with herbs and spices for a delicious meal.

Garum: Fermented fish sauce used as a condiment in various dishes.

Ingredients and Preparation:

- Fish: Garum was typically made from small fish such as anchovies, mackerel, or sardines. Sometimes fish guts and blood were also included.
- Salt: A significant amount of salt was used in the fermentation process, aiding in preservation and flavor development.
- Herbs and Spices: Some recipes might have included herbs and spices for additional flavoring.

Fermentation Process:

1. Mixing: Fish were packed in layers with salt in large containers or amphorae.
2. Fermentation: The mixture was left to ferment in the sun for several weeks to months. During this time, enzymes and bacteria would break down the fish, resulting in a pungent liquid.
3. Straining: After fermentation, the liquid was strained to remove solids, resulting in a clear, amber-colored fish sauce.

Uses in Cooking:

- Condiment: Garum was primarily used as a condiment to flavor and season dishes. It was rich in umami and added depth to various recipes.
- Seasoning: Roman cooks used garum in place of salt to season soups, stews, sauces, and meats.
- Versatility: Garum was a versatile ingredient and could be paired with a wide range of foods, including vegetables, meats, and seafood.
- Status Symbol: Depending on the quality and origin of the garum, it could be a luxury item and a status symbol among the Romans.

Variations and Similar Products:

- Muria: Another type of fish sauce similar to garum but made from a different fermentation process.
- Liquamen: Another name used for fish sauce in Roman texts, likely referring to a similar product.

Garum was a fundamental element of Roman cuisine, and its production and consumption were widespread throughout the Roman Empire. It exemplifies the Roman culinary tradition of using fermented fish products to enhance flavors and create unique tastes in their dishes.

Libum: Roman cheesecake made with flour, cheese, eggs, and honey.

Ingredients:

- 250 grams (about 1 1/4 cups) fine wheat flour (spelt flour can be used for authenticity)
- 250 grams (about 1 cup) soft cheese, such as ricotta or fresh goat cheese
- 1 egg
- A pinch of salt
- Honey, for drizzling

Instructions:

1. Preheat the Oven: Preheat your oven to 200°C (about 390°F).
2. Mix the Ingredients: In a bowl, combine the flour, soft cheese, egg, and a pinch of salt. Mix until you form a soft dough. You can use a wooden spoon or your hands to combine the ingredients.
3. Shape the Dough: On a lightly floured surface, shape the dough into small round cakes, about the size of a palm.
4. Bake the Libum: Place the shaped dough on a baking sheet lined with parchment paper. Bake in the preheated oven for about 20-25 minutes or until golden brown and cooked through.
5. Serve: Once baked, remove the libum from the oven and let them cool slightly. Drizzle honey over the top for added sweetness.
6. Enjoy: Libum can be enjoyed warm or at room temperature. Serve as a dessert or snack.

Libum was a popular sweet treat in ancient Rome, often offered as a religious offering or enjoyed at festive occasions. The simplicity of its ingredients and preparation makes it a delightful example of ancient Roman baking. The addition of honey adds a touch of sweetness to complement the richness of the cheese and flour. Try making this ancient Roman cheesecake for a taste of history!

Moretum: Cheese spread with garlic, herbs, and olive oil.

Ingredients:

- 250 grams (about 1 1/4 cups) fine wheat flour (spelt flour can be used for authenticity)
- 250 grams (about 1 cup) soft cheese, such as ricotta or fresh goat cheese
- 1 egg
- A pinch of salt
- Honey, for drizzling

Instructions:

1. Preheat the Oven: Preheat your oven to 200°C (about 390°F).
2. Mix the Ingredients: In a bowl, combine the flour, soft cheese, egg, and a pinch of salt. Mix until you form a soft dough. You can use a wooden spoon or your hands to combine the ingredients.
3. Shape the Dough: On a lightly floured surface, shape the dough into small round cakes, about the size of a palm.
4. Bake the Libum: Place the shaped dough on a baking sheet lined with parchment paper. Bake in the preheated oven for about 20-25 minutes or until golden brown and cooked through.
5. Serve: Once baked, remove the libum from the oven and let them cool slightly. Drizzle honey over the top for added sweetness.
6. Enjoy: Libum can be enjoyed warm or at room temperature. Serve as a dessert or snack.

Libum was a popular sweet treat in ancient Rome, often offered as a religious offering or enjoyed at festive occasions. The simplicity of its ingredients and preparation makes it a delightful example of ancient Roman baking. The addition of honey adds a touch of sweetness to complement the richness of the cheese and flour. Try making this ancient Roman cheesecake for a taste of history!

Moretum: Cheese spread with garlic, herbs, and olive oil.

Moretum is a traditional Roman cheese spread made with garlic, herbs, and olive oil. It was a popular accompaniment to bread and a staple in ancient Roman cuisine. Here's how to prepare Moretum:

Ingredients:

- 200 grams (about 7 ounces) of fresh cheese, such as ricotta or a soft goat cheese
- 2 cloves of garlic, minced
- A handful of fresh herbs, such as parsley, basil, or mint
- 2 tablespoons of extra virgin olive oil
- Salt and pepper, to taste

Instructions:

1. Prepare the Ingredients: Finely chop the fresh herbs and mince the garlic cloves.
2. Combine the Ingredients: In a bowl, mash the fresh cheese with a fork until smooth. Add the minced garlic, chopped herbs, olive oil, salt, and pepper to the cheese. Mix everything together until well combined.
3. Adjust Seasoning: Taste the Moretum and adjust the seasoning with additional salt or pepper if needed.
4. Serve: Transfer the Moretum to a serving bowl. Drizzle a bit of extra olive oil on top for presentation.
5. Enjoy: Serve the Moretum as a spread on slices of rustic bread or crackers. It can also be used as a dip for vegetables or as a flavorful topping for roasted meats.

Moretum was a simple yet flavorful dish enjoyed by the ancient Romans. The combination of creamy cheese, pungent garlic, fresh herbs, and fruity olive oil creates a delicious spread that highlights the essence of Mediterranean flavors. This recipe offers a taste of ancient Roman culinary heritage and can be easily recreated in modern kitchens for a delightful appetizer or snack.

Isicia Omentata: Spiced beef or pork patties grilled or fried.

Ingredients:

- 500 grams (about 1 pound) ground beef or pork
- 1 small onion, finely chopped
- 2 cloves garlic, minced
- 1-2 teaspoons ground cumin
- 1-2 teaspoons ground black pepper
- Pinch of ground coriander
- Pinch of ground allspice
- Pinch of salt
- Olive oil, for frying

Instructions:

1. Prepare the Meat Mixture: In a bowl, combine the ground beef or pork with the finely chopped onion and minced garlic.
2. Add Spices: Add the ground cumin, black pepper, ground coriander, allspice, and a pinch of salt to the meat mixture. Adjust the amount of spices based on your taste preferences.
3. Mix Thoroughly: Use your hands to mix the meat and spices together until well combined. Ensure that the spices are evenly distributed throughout the mixture.
4. Form Patties: Divide the meat mixture into equal portions and shape them into round patties, about 1/2 to 3/4 inch thick.
5. Cooking Methods:
    - Grilling: Preheat a grill or grill pan over medium-high heat. Brush the patties with a little olive oil and grill for 4-5 minutes on each side, or until cooked through.
    - Frying: Heat a frying pan over medium heat and add a bit of olive oil. Fry the patties for 4-5 minutes on each side, or until nicely browned and cooked through.
6. Serve: Once cooked, transfer the Isicia Omentata patties to a serving plate. They can be served hot as a main dish or as part of a larger Roman-inspired meal.

Isicia Omentata was a popular dish in ancient Roman times, enjoyed for its simplicity and bold flavors. The combination of aromatic spices with the savory meat creates a satisfying and flavorful dish that can be adapted to modern tastes. Serve these spiced beef or pork patties alongside vegetables, bread, or other Roman-inspired sides for a delightful meal reminiscent of ancient Rome.

Patina: Savory baked dishes made with eggs, meat, and vegetables.

Ingredients:

- 6 eggs
- 200 grams (about 7 ounces) cooked meat (such as chicken, pork, or beef), diced or shredded
- 1 cup cooked vegetables (such as spinach, asparagus, or mushrooms), chopped
- 50 grams (about 1/2 cup) grated cheese (such as Parmesan or pecorino), optional
- 2 tablespoons fresh herbs (such as parsley, basil, or thyme), chopped
- Salt and pepper, to taste
- Olive oil or butter, for greasing

Instructions:

1. Preheat the Oven: Preheat your oven to 350°F (175°C).
2. Prepare the Ingredients: Cook and prepare the meat and vegetables if they are not already cooked. Dice or shred the cooked meat, and chop the cooked vegetables into bite-sized pieces.
3. Whisk the Eggs: In a mixing bowl, whisk the eggs until well beaten. Season with salt and pepper.
4. Combine Ingredients: Add the cooked meat, vegetables, grated cheese (if using), and chopped herbs to the beaten eggs. Mix everything together until well combined.
5. Grease a Baking Dish: Grease a baking dish (a shallow casserole dish or pie dish works well) with olive oil or butter to prevent sticking.
6. Pour the Mixture: Pour the egg and ingredient mixture into the greased baking dish, spreading it out evenly.
7. Bake: Place the baking dish in the preheated oven and bake for about 20-25 minutes, or until the patina is set and the top is golden brown.
8. Serve: Remove the patina from the oven and let it cool slightly. Cut into slices or squares and serve warm.
9. Variations: Feel free to customize your patina with different meats, vegetables, cheeses, or herbs based on your preferences and what ingredients are available. You can also add spices or seasonings for additional flavor.

Patina was a versatile dish in ancient Rome and could be served as a main course or a side dish. It showcases the use of simple ingredients combined with eggs to create a satisfying and flavorful baked dish. Enjoy this historical recipe as a connection to the culinary traditions of ancient Rome!

Gustum: Appetizers served before the main course.

Gustum Dishes:

1. Olives: Marinated olives were a popular and simple gustum dish, providing a salty and flavorful start to the meal.
2. Cheese Platter: Assorted cheeses, such as aged pecorino or fresh ricotta, served with bread or honey, were a delightful gustum offering.
3. Cold Meats: Slices of cured or smoked meats, such as salami or prosciutto, were often served as gustum to whet the appetite.
4. Stuffed Vegetables: Small stuffed vegetables like mushrooms or peppers filled with seasoned breadcrumbs, cheese, and herbs made for tasty gustum bites.
5. Shellfish: Fresh or marinated shellfish, such as mussels or oysters, were enjoyed as gustum, especially in coastal regions.
6. Egg Dishes: Dishes like omelets or scrambled eggs with herbs and cheese were served as gustum, providing protein and flavor.
7. Fritters: Fried fritters made from vegetables, fish, or cheese were common gustum offerings, crispy and satisfying.
8. Nuts and Dried Fruits: Almonds, walnuts, and dried figs or dates were often served as a simple and nutritious gustum.
9. Sauces and Dips: Various dips and sauces, such as garum-based sauces or olive oil with herbs, accompanied bread or vegetables as gustum.

Serving Gustum:

- Gustum dishes were typically served on small plates or platters and placed on the table for diners to enjoy before the main meal.
- These appetizers were meant to be light and flavorful, setting the stage for the courses to follow.
- The selection of gustum dishes varied depending on the occasion, the season, and the preferences of the host and guests.

Understanding gustum in ancient Roman dining provides insight into the culinary customs and appreciation for appetizing starters that have influenced dining traditions throughout history. These small and flavorful dishes were an essential part of the dining experience, encouraging social interaction and enjoyment before the main course was served.

Ova Spongia ex Lacte: Egg custard with milk and honey.

Ingredients:

- 4 eggs
- 1 cup milk (you can use cow's milk or goat's milk)
- 2-3 tablespoons honey (adjust to taste)
- A pinch of ground cinnamon (optional)
- A pinch of ground nutmeg (optional)
- A splash of vanilla extract (optional)
- Butter or olive oil, for greasing

Instructions:

1. Preheat the Oven: Preheat your oven to 350°F (175°C).
2. Prepare the Custard Mixture: In a mixing bowl, crack the eggs and whisk them until well beaten.
3. Sweeten the Mixture: Add the milk, honey, and any optional flavorings (such as cinnamon, nutmeg, or vanilla extract) to the beaten eggs. Whisk everything together until well combined.
4. Grease a Baking Dish: Grease a baking dish (a pie dish or shallow casserole dish works well) with butter or olive oil to prevent sticking.
5. Pour the Mixture: Pour the egg and milk mixture into the greased baking dish.
6. Bake the Custard: Place the baking dish in the preheated oven and bake for about 30-35 minutes, or until the custard is set and the top is golden brown.
7. Serve: Remove the custard from the oven and let it cool slightly. Cut into slices or squares and serve warm or at room temperature.
8. Optional Garnish: You can garnish the Ova Spongia ex Lacte with a drizzle of honey or a sprinkle of ground cinnamon before serving.

This Roman-style egg custard is a simple and comforting dessert that showcases the use of basic ingredients like eggs, milk, and honey to create a satisfying sweet dish. The addition of spices like cinnamon and nutmeg adds warmth and flavor to the custard. Enjoy this historical recipe as a delightful taste of ancient Roman cuisine!

Mellaria: Honey-based desserts and sweets.

Honey-Based Desserts and Sweets:

1. Honey Cakes: Simple cakes or breads sweetened with honey and flavored with spices like cinnamon and nutmeg.
2. Honey Nut Pastries: Pastries filled with a mixture of honey and chopped nuts (such as almonds or walnuts).
3. Honey Fritters: Deep-fried doughnuts or fritters coated in honey syrup.
4. Honeyed Fruits: Fresh fruits (like figs, dates, or pears) poached in honey syrup and served as a sweet treat.
5. Honey Custard: Creamy custard sweetened with honey and flavored with vanilla or spices.
6. Honey Nut Bars: Bars made from a mixture of nuts, seeds, and honey, pressed together and cut into squares.
7. Honeyed Wine Jellies: Gelatin desserts flavored with sweetened wine and honey.
8. Honey-Sweetened Yogurt or Cheese: Soft cheeses or yogurt drizzled with honey for a sweet and creamy dessert.

Ingredients for Making Mellaria:

- Honey (locally sourced honey was highly valued in ancient Rome)
- Flour (for cakes and pastries)
- Nuts (such as almonds, walnuts, or pine nuts)
- Spices (like cinnamon, nutmeg, or cloves)
- Fruits (fresh or dried fruits like figs, dates, or apples)
- Eggs (for custards and baked goods)
- Wine (for flavoring jellies and desserts)

Preparation Methods:

- Mixing: Combining honey with other ingredients like flour, nuts, and spices to create doughs or batters.
- Baking: Baking honey-sweetened cakes, breads, and pastries in clay ovens.
- Frying: Deep-frying doughnuts or fritters and then coating them with honey syrup.
- Poaching: Simmering fruits in a honey syrup until they are tender and sweet.

Honey was not only used as a sweetener but also valued for its medicinal properties

and symbolic significance in Roman culture. Mellaria represented a delightful array of desserts and sweets enjoyed by the ancient Romans, showcasing the versatility and deliciousness of honey in culinary creations.

Laganum: Thin flatbread often served with cheese and honey.

Ingredients for Laganum (Thin Flatbread):

- 1 cup all-purpose flour
- 1/2 cup water
- Pinch of salt
- Olive oil, for cooking

Instructions:

1. Make the Dough: In a mixing bowl, combine the flour and salt. Gradually add the water, stirring continuously, until a smooth dough forms.
2. Knead the Dough: Transfer the dough onto a lightly floured surface and knead for about 5-7 minutes until it becomes elastic and smooth.
3. Rest the Dough: Place the dough back into the mixing bowl, cover with a kitchen towel, and let it rest for about 30 minutes.
4. Divide the Dough: After resting, divide the dough into small balls (about the size of a golf ball).
5. Roll Out the Dough: Take one dough ball at a time and roll it out on a lightly floured surface into a thin round flatbread (about 6-8 inches in diameter).
6. Cook the Laganum: Heat a non-stick skillet or frying pan over medium-high heat. Brush the pan with a little olive oil. Cook each flatbread for about 1-2 minutes on each side until lightly browned and cooked through. Repeat with the remaining dough balls.
7. Serve the Laganum: Serve the cooked laganum warm with toppings of your choice.

Serving Suggestions with Cheese and Honey:

- Cheese and Honey Laganum: Spread a thin layer of fresh ricotta cheese or soft goat cheese on a warm laganum. Drizzle with honey over the cheese.
- Additional Toppings: You can enhance the laganum with additional toppings like chopped nuts (such as walnuts or almonds), fresh herbs (such as thyme or rosemary), or a sprinkle of ground cinnamon.

Laganum was a versatile staple in ancient Roman cuisine, enjoyed both as a simple bread and as a base for various toppings. The combination of cheese and honey on laganum provided a delicious blend of savory and sweet flavors, reflecting the culinary preferences of ancient Roman dining. Experiment with different toppings and flavors to create your own version of this historical dish!

Pullum Numidicum: Chicken cooked with spices and apricots.

Ingredients:

- 4 chicken thighs or breasts, bone-in and skin-on
- 1 onion, finely chopped
- 2 cloves garlic, minced
- 1 teaspoon ground cumin
- 1 teaspoon ground coriander
- 1/2 teaspoon ground cinnamon
- 1/4 teaspoon ground ginger
- Salt and pepper, to taste
- 1 cup dried apricots, halved
- 1 cup chicken broth or water
- Olive oil
- Fresh parsley or cilantro, chopped (for garnish)

Instructions:

1. Prepare the Chicken: Season the chicken pieces with salt and pepper.
2. Sear the Chicken: Heat some olive oil in a large skillet or Dutch oven over medium-high heat. Add the chicken pieces, skin side down, and cook until browned and crispy, about 5-6 minutes per side. Remove the chicken from the pan and set aside.
3. Cook the Aromatics: In the same pan, add a bit more olive oil if needed. Add the chopped onion and sauté until softened, about 3-4 minutes. Add the minced garlic and cook for another 1-2 minutes until fragrant.
4. Add Spices: Stir in the ground cumin, coriander, cinnamon, ginger, salt, and pepper. Cook for a minute or so until the spices are toasted and aromatic.
5. Combine with Apricots and Liquid: Add the dried apricots to the pan, along with the chicken broth or water. Stir to combine and bring to a simmer.
6. Simmer the Chicken: Return the chicken pieces to the pan, nestling them into the apricot and spice mixture. Cover the pan and let it simmer gently for about 20-25 minutes, or until the chicken is cooked through and tender, and the apricots are softened.
7. Adjust Seasoning: Taste and adjust the seasoning with salt and pepper if needed.
8. Serve: Transfer the Pullum Numidicum to a serving dish. Garnish with chopped parsley or cilantro.
9. Enjoy: Serve the chicken and apricot stew hot, accompanied by couscous, rice, or crusty bread to soak up the flavorful sauce.

Pullum Numidicum reflects the Roman culinary practice of incorporating spices and dried fruits into savory dishes, influenced by the flavors of North Africa. This aromatic and flavorful chicken dish would have been a delightful addition to a Roman banquet or family meal, showcasing the diverse and exotic ingredients enjoyed in ancient times.

Conditurae: Various sauces and relishes used to flavor dishes.

Types of Conditurae:

1. Garum: A fermented fish sauce made from fish or fish guts, salt, and sometimes herbs. Garum was used extensively as a condiment to season various dishes.
2. Salsa: A general term for sauces or relishes made from a variety of ingredients, such as herbs, spices, vinegar, and sometimes fruits or vegetables.
3. Ius: A sauce or gravy made from meat drippings, wine, and herbs, used to dress and flavor meats and other dishes.
4. Oenogarum: A mixture of garum (fish sauce) and wine, used as a dipping sauce or dressing.
5. Defrutum: A thick syrup made from reduced grape juice, used as a sweetener and flavoring agent in sauces and desserts.
6. Mentum: A sauce made from honey, vinegar, and various herbs and spices, used to flavor meats and vegetables.
7. Allec: A sauce made from garlic, vinegar, and sometimes herbs, used as a condiment or flavoring.
8. Sapa: Another type of grape syrup made from reduced grape juice, similar to defrutum.

Uses of Conditurae:

- Flavoring Meats: Conditurae were used to season and marinate meats before cooking or as a sauce to accompany cooked meats.
- Enhancing Vegetables: They were used to dress and flavor vegetables, making them more palatable and flavorful.
- Dipping Sauces: Some conditurae, like oenogarum or allec, were used as dipping sauces for bread or other foods.
- Preserving Foods: Conditurae containing vinegar or fermented ingredients helped preserve foods and extend their shelf life.
- Dessert Flavorings: Sweet conditurae like defrutum or sapa were used to sweeten and flavor desserts and sweet dishes.

Conditurae were integral to ancient Roman cooking, reflecting a sophisticated understanding of flavor combinations and culinary techniques. They demonstrate the Romans' skill in using a variety of ingredients to create complex and delicious sauces and relishes that added richness and character to their meals.

Fungi: Mushrooms used in various dishes.

Uses of Mushrooms (Fungi) in Ancient Roman Cuisine:

1. Cooked in Stews and Sauces: Mushrooms were often added to meat or vegetable stews to enhance flavor and texture. They were also used in sauces to accompany roasted meats or pasta dishes.
2. Stuffed Mushrooms: Large mushrooms, such as portobello or field mushrooms, were stuffed with a mixture of breadcrumbs, herbs, cheese, and sometimes minced meat before baking or grilling.
3. In Omelets and Frittatas: Mushrooms were a popular filling for omelets and frittatas, providing a savory and earthy flavor.
4. Mushroom Pastries: Mushrooms were combined with cheese or herbs and enclosed in pastry dough to create savory mushroom-filled pastries or pies.
5. Mushroom Soups: Mushrooms were simmered with broth, vegetables, and herbs to create hearty and flavorful mushroom soups.
6. Pickled Mushrooms: Mushrooms were sometimes pickled in vinegar and spices for preservation and served as appetizers or side dishes.
7. Sautéed Mushrooms: Mushrooms were frequently sautéed with garlic, herbs, and olive oil as a simple and delicious side dish.
8. Mushroom Salads: Sliced raw mushrooms were used in salads, often paired with fresh greens, herbs, and a vinaigrette dressing.

Popular Mushroom Varieties Used in Ancient Rome:

- Boletus: A type of wild mushroom appreciated for its meaty texture and rich flavor.
- Chanterelle: Known for its fruity aroma and delicate flavor, chanterelle mushrooms were prized by the Romans.
- Porcini: Another type of wild mushroom highly valued for its robust flavor and earthy notes.
- Button Mushrooms: Common cultivated mushrooms used in various dishes due to their mild flavor and versatility.
- Morels: These unique mushrooms with a distinctive honeycomb texture were considered a delicacy in ancient Rome.

Culinary Significance:

Mushrooms held a special place in ancient Roman cuisine, offering a range of flavors and textures that complemented other ingredients. They were valued for their umami-rich taste and were used in both simple and elaborate dishes, showcasing the Romans' appreciation for diverse and flavorful ingredients in their cooking. Today, mushrooms continue to be cherished for their culinary versatility and nutritional benefits, carrying on a tradition that dates back to ancient times.

Gustum de Praecoquis: Dessert made with stewed quinces and honey.

Ingredients:

- 2-3 quinces, peeled, cored, and diced
- 1 cup water
- 1/2 cup honey (adjust to taste)
- 1 cinnamon stick
- Pinch of ground cloves
- Pinch of ground black pepper
- Fresh mint leaves, for garnish (optional)

Instructions:

1. Prepare the Quinces: Peel the quinces, remove the cores, and dice them into small pieces.
2. Stew the Quinces: In a saucepan, combine the diced quinces with water, honey, cinnamon stick, ground cloves, and black pepper.
3. Simmer the Mixture: Bring the mixture to a boil over medium-high heat. Then, reduce the heat to low and let it simmer gently, stirring occasionally, for about 20-25 minutes or until the quinces are tender and cooked through.
4. Check for Sweetness: Taste the stewed quinces and adjust the sweetness by adding more honey if desired.
5. Serve: Remove the cinnamon stick from the pot. Spoon the warm stewed quinces into serving bowls.
6. Garnish: If desired, garnish the dessert with fresh mint leaves for a touch of freshness and color.
7. Enjoy: Serve the Gustum de Praecoquis warm as a comforting and aromatic dessert. It can be enjoyed on its own or served with a dollop of whipped cream or a scoop of vanilla ice cream for a delightful treat.

Notes:

- Quinces have a natural tartness, which is balanced by the sweetness of honey in this dessert. Adjust the amount of honey based on your taste preferences and the sweetness of the quinces.
- The spices like cinnamon, cloves, and black pepper add warmth and depth to the dish, enhancing the flavors of the stewed quinces.
- This dessert can be prepared in advance and stored in the refrigerator. Simply reheat before serving, or enjoy it chilled as a refreshing treat.

Gustum de Praecoquis showcases the Romans' skill in using seasonal fruits and natural sweeteners like honey to create delicious and comforting desserts. Recreating this ancient Roman dish provides a delightful connection to culinary traditions of the past while celebrating the unique flavors of quinces and honey.

Pernae: Ham dishes prepared in different ways.

Ham Dishes in Ancient Roman Cuisine:

1. Roasted Ham: Whole or half hams were roasted over an open fire or in a clay oven, seasoned with herbs and spices for flavor.
2. Glazed Ham: Ham could be coated with a honey or wine glaze and roasted until caramelized, creating a sweet and savory dish.
3. Ham Slices: Thin slices of ham were served as part of appetizers or main courses, often accompanied by cheeses, bread, or fruits.
4. Ham Stew: Chunks of ham were simmered with vegetables and legumes to make hearty stews or soups.
5. Ham and Cheese Pie: Ham was combined with cheese, eggs, and herbs, then baked in pastry dough to create savory pies.
6. Ham and Vegetable Skewers: Cubes of ham were skewered with vegetables and grilled over coals, creating flavorful kebabs.
7. Ham Sausages: Ground ham meat was seasoned with herbs and spices, stuffed into casings, and cooked or smoked to make sausages.

Ingredients Used with Ham:

- Garum: A fermented fish sauce used to season and flavor ham dishes.
- Wine: Wine was often used in marinades, glazes, or sauces for ham.
- Honey: Honey was a common sweetener used to balance the saltiness of ham in various dishes.
- Herbs and Spices: Commonly used herbs and spices included black pepper, cumin, coriander, and savory herbs like thyme and rosemary.

Culinary Techniques:

- Roasting: Ham was typically roasted over an open fire or in ovens, resulting in tender and flavorful meat.
- Smoking: Ham was sometimes smoked to preserve and enhance its flavor.
- Marinating: Ham was marinated in wine, vinegar, or seasoned brines to enhance its taste and tenderness.
- Combination with Other Ingredients: Ham was often combined with cheeses, eggs, vegetables, or grains to create balanced and satisfying dishes.

Ham dishes were appreciated for their hearty and savory qualities in ancient Rome, reflecting the culinary sophistication and diverse tastes of the Roman era. Recreating these historical ham preparations provides a glimpse into the rich culinary heritage of ancient Roman cuisine.

Conditum Paradoxum: Spiced wine used as a drink or in cooking.

Ingredients for Conditum Paradoxum (Spiced Wine):

- 1 bottle of red wine (choose a medium-bodied red wine like a Merlot or Cabernet Sauvignon)
- 1 cup honey
- Zest of 1 orange
- Zest of 1 lemon
- 1 teaspoon whole black peppercorns
- 1 teaspoon whole cloves
- 1 small piece of fresh ginger, thinly sliced
- 1 cinnamon stick
- Pinch of ground nutmeg
- Pinch of ground cardamom (optional)
- Pinch of sea salt

Instructions:

1. Prepare the Spiced Wine Mixture:
    - In a large saucepan, combine the honey, orange zest, lemon zest, whole black peppercorns, whole cloves, fresh ginger slices, cinnamon stick, ground nutmeg, ground cardamom (if using), and a pinch of sea salt.
    - Pour in the red wine and stir to combine.
2. Simmer the Mixture:
    - Place the saucepan over medium-low heat and slowly bring the mixture to a gentle simmer, stirring occasionally to dissolve the honey.
    - Be careful not to boil the wine mixture; you want to gently infuse the flavors without evaporating the alcohol.
3. Infuse Flavors:
    - Let the wine mixture simmer gently for about 15-20 minutes, allowing the spices and citrus zest to infuse their flavors into the wine.
    - Taste the spiced wine mixture and adjust the sweetness or spiciness by adding more honey, spices, or a pinch of salt if needed.
4. Strain and Serve:
    - Once the spiced wine has infused to your liking, remove the saucepan from the heat.
    - Strain the Conditum Paradoxum through a fine mesh sieve or cheesecloth to remove the spices and citrus zest.

- Discard the solids and transfer the strained spiced wine into a serving pitcher or individual glasses.
5. Serve:
    - Conditum Paradoxum can be served warm or chilled, depending on your preference.
    - Garnish each serving with a fresh orange or lemon twist for an extra touch of citrus aroma.
6. Enjoy:
    - Serve this delightful spiced wine as a festive drink during gatherings or enjoy it as a unique and flavorful beverage inspired by ancient Roman cuisine.

Conditum Paradoxum was valued not only as a delicious drink but also for its supposed medicinal and aphrodisiac qualities in ancient Rome. Recreating this spiced wine recipe offers a taste of history and a delightful way to experience the flavors cherished by ancient Romans during their feasts and celebrations.

In Mitulis: Mussels cooked with herbs and wine.

Ingredients for Mussels Cooked with Herbs and Wine:

- 2 pounds fresh mussels, cleaned and debearded
- 2 tablespoons olive oil
- 3-4 garlic cloves, minced
- 1/2 cup dry white wine
- 1/4 cup chopped fresh parsley
- 1 tablespoon chopped fresh thyme (or 1 teaspoon dried thyme)
- Salt and pepper, to taste
- Pinch of crushed red pepper flakes (optional)
- Lemon wedges, for serving
- Crusty bread, for serving

Instructions:

1. Prepare the Mussels:
    - Scrub the mussels under cold running water to remove any grit or debris.
    - Debeard the mussels by pulling off the fibrous threads (called beards) protruding from the shells.
2. Cook the Mussels:
    - In a large pot or Dutch oven, heat the olive oil over medium heat.
    - Add the minced garlic and cook for about 1 minute until fragrant.
3. Add Wine and Herbs:
    - Pour in the white wine and bring it to a simmer.
    - Add the chopped parsley, thyme, salt, pepper, and crushed red pepper flakes (if using). Stir to combine.
4. Cook the Mussels:
    - Add the cleaned mussels to the pot, then cover with a lid.
    - Cook the mussels for about 5-7 minutes, shaking the pot occasionally, until the mussels have opened up.
5. Discard Unopened Mussels:
    - Discard any mussels that have not opened after cooking.
6. Serve:
    - Transfer the cooked mussels and aromatic broth to serving bowls.
    - Serve the mussels with lemon wedges on the side for squeezing over the mussels.
    - Provide crusty bread for soaking up the flavorful broth.
7. Enjoy:

- Enjoy the "In Mitulis" mussels as a delicious appetizer or main course, accompanied by a glass of white wine.

This dish of mussels cooked with herbs and wine reflects the simplicity and flavor-forward approach of ancient Roman seafood preparations. The combination of garlic, fresh herbs, and white wine enhances the natural sweetness of the mussels, creating a delightful and satisfying dish reminiscent of ancient Roman coastal cuisine.

Gustum de Castaneis: Sweet chestnut dessert.

Ingredients for Gustum de Castaneis (Sweet Chestnut Dessert):

- 1 pound fresh chestnuts
- 1 cup water
- 1 cup honey
- 1 cinnamon stick
- Zest of 1 lemon
- Pinch of salt
- Optional: Ground cinnamon or powdered sugar for garnish

Instructions:

1. Prepare the Chestnuts:
    - Using a sharp knife, carefully score an "X" on the flat side of each chestnut.
    - Place the chestnuts in a pot of boiling water and blanch for about 5 minutes.
    - Remove the chestnuts from the water and let them cool slightly.
    - Peel off the outer shell and inner skin (pellicle) from the chestnuts. This step can be easier when the chestnuts are still warm.
2. Cook the Chestnuts:
    - In a saucepan, combine the peeled chestnuts with 1 cup of water.
    - Add the honey, cinnamon stick, lemon zest, and a pinch of salt to the saucepan.
3. Simmer the Mixture:
    - Bring the chestnut mixture to a simmer over medium heat.
    - Reduce the heat to low and let it simmer gently, stirring occasionally, for about 20-25 minutes or until the chestnuts are tender and the liquid has thickened into a syrupy consistency.
4. Mash or Purée:
    - Use a fork or potato masher to mash the cooked chestnuts into a coarse paste or purée. You can leave some texture for added interest.
5. Serve:
    - Transfer the sweet chestnut mixture to a serving dish or individual bowls.
    - Optionally, sprinkle ground cinnamon or powdered sugar on top for garnish.
6. Enjoy:

- Serve the Gustum de Castaneis warm or at room temperature as a delightful and comforting dessert.

This sweet chestnut dessert reflects the ancient Roman appreciation for chestnuts as a delicious and nutritious ingredient. The combination of honey, cinnamon, and lemon zest enhances the natural sweetness of the chestnuts, creating a satisfying and flavorful treat that would have been enjoyed by Romans in antiquity. Recreating this ancient-inspired dessert offers a taste of history and a connection to the culinary traditions of the past.

Minutal Matianum: Stew made with pork, chicken, or fish.

Ingredients for Minutal Matianum Stew:

- 1 pound pork shoulder or pork loin, cut into bite-sized pieces
- 1 pound chicken thighs or breasts, cut into bite-sized pieces (or substitute with fish fillets if preferred)
- 2 tablespoons olive oil
- 1 onion, chopped
- 2 garlic cloves, minced
- 2 carrots, peeled and sliced
- 2 celery stalks, sliced
- 1 bell pepper, diced
- 1 zucchini, diced
- 1 cup cherry tomatoes, halved
- 1 cup chicken or vegetable broth
- 1/2 cup white wine
- 1 teaspoon dried oregano
- 1 teaspoon dried thyme
- Salt and pepper, to taste
- Fresh parsley, chopped, for garnish

Instructions:

1. Sear the Meat:
   - In a large pot or Dutch oven, heat the olive oil over medium-high heat.
   - Add the pork and chicken pieces to the pot, and sear until browned on all sides. If using fish, skip this step and add it later to avoid overcooking.
2. Add Aromatics and Vegetables:
   - Add the chopped onion, minced garlic, carrots, celery, bell pepper, and zucchini to the pot.
   - Sauté for about 5 minutes until the vegetables start to soften.
3. Deglaze with Wine:
   - Pour in the white wine to deglaze the pot, scraping up any browned bits from the bottom.
4. Simmer the Stew:
   - Add the cherry tomatoes, chicken or vegetable broth, dried oregano, dried thyme, salt, and pepper to the pot.
   - Bring the stew to a simmer, then reduce the heat to low.

- Cover and let the stew simmer gently for about 30-40 minutes, or until the pork and chicken are tender and cooked through.
5. Adjust Seasoning:
    - Taste the stew and adjust the seasoning with salt and pepper if needed.
6. Serve:
    - Ladle the Minutal Matianum stew into bowls.
    - Garnish with chopped fresh parsley for a pop of color and freshness.
7. Enjoy:
    - Serve the hearty Minutal Matianum stew hot, accompanied by crusty bread or cooked grains like rice or barley.

This Minutal Matianum stew represents the robust and flavorful dishes enjoyed by the ancient Romans, combining meat or fish with an array of vegetables and aromatic seasonings. Recreating this ancient-inspired stew offers a taste of Roman culinary heritage and celebrates the diversity of ingredients used in ancient Roman cooking. Adjust the ingredients based on availability and personal preference to create a satisfying and delicious meal reminiscent of ancient times.

Caponata: Eggplant-based dish with vinegar and other vegetables.

Ingredients for Caponata:

- 1 large eggplant, cut into cubes
- Salt, for sweating the eggplant
- Olive oil, for frying
- 1 onion, finely chopped
- 2 celery stalks, diced
- 1 red bell pepper, diced
- 1 can (14 oz) diced tomatoes, drained
- 2-3 tablespoons capers, drained
- 1/4 cup green olives, pitted and sliced
- 3 tablespoons red wine vinegar
- 1-2 tablespoons sugar (adjust to taste)
- Salt and black pepper, to taste
- Fresh basil leaves, chopped (optional)

Instructions:

1. Prepare the Eggplant:
    - Place the eggplant cubes in a colander, sprinkle with salt, and let them sit for about 30 minutes. This helps draw out excess moisture and bitterness from the eggplant. Rinse and pat dry with paper towels.
2. Fry the Eggplant:
    - In a large skillet, heat olive oil over medium-high heat.
    - Add the eggplant cubes in batches and fry until golden brown and tender. Remove and drain on paper towels.
3. Cook the Vegetables:
    - In the same skillet, add a bit more olive oil if needed. Sauté the chopped onion, celery, and red bell pepper until softened, about 5-7 minutes.
4. Combine Ingredients:
    - Add the diced tomatoes, capers, and sliced olives to the skillet. Stir to combine.
5. Simmer with Vinegar and Sugar:
    - Pour in the red wine vinegar and sprinkle with sugar (adjust to taste).
    - Season with salt and black pepper. Stir well to incorporate all ingredients.
6. Add Fried Eggplant:
    - Gently add the fried eggplant cubes to the skillet, stirring carefully to combine with the other ingredients.

7. Simmer and Adjust Seasoning:
   - Reduce the heat to low and let the caponata simmer gently for about 15-20 minutes to allow the flavors to meld together.
   - Taste and adjust the seasoning with salt, pepper, and additional sugar or vinegar if needed.
8. Serve:
   - Transfer the caponata to a serving dish.
   - Garnish with chopped fresh basil leaves, if desired.
9. Enjoy:
   - Serve the caponata warm or at room temperature as a delicious appetizer, side dish, or topping for crusty bread.

Caponata is a versatile dish that can be enjoyed on its own, served as a side dish, or used as a topping for bruschetta or pasta. Its combination of sweet, savory, and tangy flavors makes it a delightful representation of Mediterranean cuisine and a nod to the historical culinary influences of ancient Rome in the region.

Laganophila: Lamb or pork dishes wrapped in dough and baked.

Ingredients for Laganophila (Meat Wrapped in Dough):

For the Filling:

- 1 pound lamb or pork shoulder, diced into small pieces
- 1 onion, finely chopped
- 2 cloves garlic, minced
- 1 teaspoon dried oregano
- Salt and pepper, to taste
- Olive oil, for cooking

For the Dough:

- 2 cups all-purpose flour
- 1 teaspoon salt
- 1/2 cup water
- 1/4 cup olive oil

Instructions:

1. Prepare the Filling:
    - In a skillet, heat olive oil over medium heat.
    - Add the chopped onion and minced garlic, and sauté until softened and translucent.
    - Add the diced lamb or pork to the skillet and cook until browned on all sides.
    - Season with dried oregano, salt, and pepper. Remove from heat and let the filling mixture cool slightly.
2. Make the Dough:
    - In a mixing bowl, combine the flour and salt.
    - Gradually add the water and olive oil, mixing until a dough forms.
    - Knead the dough on a lightly floured surface until smooth and elastic. Cover with a kitchen towel and let it rest for about 30 minutes.
3. Assemble the Laganophila:
    - Preheat your oven to 375°F (190°C).
    - Divide the dough into small portions and roll each portion into a thin circle or oval shape, about 1/8 inch thick.
4. Fill and Wrap:

- Place a spoonful of the cooked meat filling onto one half of each dough circle.
- Fold the other half of the dough over the filling to enclose it, then crimp the edges to seal.

5. Bake:
   - Place the filled and sealed dough parcels on a baking sheet lined with parchment paper.
   - Bake in the preheated oven for about 20-25 minutes, or until the dough is golden brown and cooked through.
6. Serve:
   - Remove the laganophila from the oven and let them cool slightly.
   - Serve warm as a delicious and hearty main dish or appetizer.

Variations and Tips:

- Seasoning: Feel free to customize the filling with additional herbs, spices, or vegetables according to your taste preferences.
- Meat Options: While lamb or pork are traditional choices, you can use other meats such as beef, chicken, or even vegetarian fillings with cheese and vegetables.
- Dough Texture: Adjust the dough consistency as needed by adding more flour or water to achieve a workable dough.

Laganophila represents the ancient Roman tradition of combining meat and dough in a comforting and satisfying dish. This recipe provides a modern interpretation of this historical concept, allowing you to enjoy a taste of ancient Roman cuisine with a delicious meat-filled pastry.

Patella: Omelette or quiche-like dish with various ingredients.

Ingredients for Patella (Ancient Roman Omelette/Quiche):

- 6 large eggs
- 1/2 cup milk or cream
- 1 cup diced cooked ham or cooked sausage (optional)
- 1 cup diced vegetables (e.g., bell peppers, onions, spinach, mushrooms)
- 1/2 cup grated cheese (e.g., Parmesan, Cheddar, or feta)
- 2 tablespoons chopped fresh herbs (e.g., parsley, basil, or thyme)
- Salt and pepper, to taste
- Olive oil or butter, for cooking

Instructions:

1. Preheat the Oven:
    - Preheat your oven to 350°F (175°C).
2. Prepare the Filling:
    - In a skillet, heat some olive oil or butter over medium heat.
    - Add the diced vegetables and cook until softened, about 5-7 minutes.
    - If using ham or sausage, add it to the skillet and cook briefly until heated through.
    - Remove from heat and let the filling mixture cool slightly.
3. Whisk the Eggs:
    - In a mixing bowl, whisk together the eggs, milk or cream, chopped fresh herbs, salt, and pepper until well combined.
4. Assemble the Patella:
    - Grease a baking dish or pie dish with olive oil or butter.
    - Spread the cooked vegetable and meat mixture evenly over the bottom of the dish.
    - Sprinkle grated cheese on top of the filling.
5. Pour in the Egg Mixture:
    - Slowly pour the egg mixture over the filling in the baking dish.
6. Bake the Patella:
    - Place the baking dish in the preheated oven and bake for 25-30 minutes, or until the eggs are set and the top is golden brown.
7. Serve:
    - Remove the patella from the oven and let it cool for a few minutes.
    - Slice into wedges or squares and serve warm as a delicious main dish or side dish.

Variations and Tips:

- Vegetarian Option: Omit the meat and use additional vegetables or cheese for a vegetarian version of patella.
- Customize the Ingredients: Feel free to use your favorite vegetables, meats, cheeses, and herbs based on availability and preference.
- Make-Ahead: You can prepare the filling and egg mixture in advance, then assemble and bake the patella when ready to serve.

Patella is a versatile and satisfying dish that reflects the ancient Roman tradition of combining ingredients into a hearty egg-based meal. This recipe allows you to recreate the concept of patella with a modern twist, making it a delightful option for breakfast, brunch, or any meal of the day. Adjust the ingredients and flavors to suit your taste and enjoy exploring the culinary heritage of ancient Rome through this delicious dish.

Gustum de Cerebellis: Dessert made with spelt and honey.

Ingredients for Gustum de Cerebellis (Spelt and Honey Dessert):

- 1 cup spelt grains (also known as farro)
- 3 cups water
- 1/4 teaspoon salt
- 1/4 cup honey (plus more for drizzling)
- Ground cinnamon, for garnish (optional)
- Chopped nuts (e.g., almonds, walnuts), for garnish (optional)

Instructions:

1. Cook the Spelt:
   - In a saucepan, combine the spelt grains, water, and salt.
   - Bring to a boil over medium-high heat, then reduce the heat to low and simmer gently for about 25-30 minutes, or until the spelt grains are tender but still chewy.
   - Drain any excess water from the cooked spelt.
2. Sweeten with Honey:
   - Transfer the cooked spelt grains to a mixing bowl.
   - Drizzle the honey over the spelt grains, stirring gently to coat the grains evenly with honey.
3. Serve:
   - Spoon the sweetened spelt grains into serving bowls or plates.
4. Garnish:
   - Optionally, sprinkle ground cinnamon over the top for added flavor and aroma.
   - Garnish with chopped nuts such as almonds or walnuts for texture and crunch.
5. Enjoy:
   - Serve the Gustum de Cerebellis warm or at room temperature as a simple and wholesome dessert.

Variations and Tips:

- Additions: Feel free to customize this dessert by adding dried fruits (e.g., raisins, chopped dates), citrus zest, or a splash of citrus juice for extra flavor.
- Texture: Adjust the cooking time of the spelt grains to achieve your desired texture—some prefer a softer texture while others prefer a chewier texture.

- Presentation: Serve this dessert as a rustic dish in individual bowls or on a platter, garnished with a drizzle of honey and a sprinkle of cinnamon for a beautiful presentation.

Gustum de Cerebellis represents the ancient Roman use of spelt and honey in creating simple yet delightful desserts. This recipe offers a glimpse into the culinary heritage of ancient Rome, showcasing the use of wholesome ingredients to create satisfying and naturally sweet dishes. Enjoy this ancient-inspired dessert as a nutritious and flavorful treat!

Vitella: Veal dishes cooked in different styles.

Examples of Vitella (Veal Dishes):

1. Vitella Conditum: Veal cooked with a spiced sauce or marinade, possibly using ingredients like wine, vinegar, honey, herbs, and spices.
2. Vitella Assa: Roasted veal, seasoned with herbs and spices, and cooked over an open fire or in a clay oven.
3. Vitella Fricata: Veal cutlets or slices pan-fried or grilled, served with a savory sauce or relish.
4. Vitella In Patina: Veal cooked in a casserole dish or mold with other ingredients such as eggs, cheese, vegetables, and herbs, similar to a savory custard or baked dish.
5. Vitella Concia: Marinated veal, often with garlic, vinegar, olive oil, and herbs, then grilled or sautéed.
6. Vitella Farsilis: Veal stuffing or meatballs made with seasoned ground veal, breadcrumbs, eggs, and herbs, either baked or simmered in a sauce.

Ingredients Used with Vitella:

- Wine and Vinegar: Commonly used for marinating and flavoring veal dishes.
- Honey: Used as a sweetener in sauces or marinades for veal.
- Herbs and Spices: Including bay leaves, black pepper, cumin, coriander, rue, lovage, and more, to enhance flavor.
- Cheese: Sometimes incorporated into veal dishes, either as a topping or in fillings.

Culinary Techniques for Cooking Vitella:

- Roasting: Veal was often roasted over an open fire or in ovens.
- Grilling and Sautéing: Veal cutlets or slices were cooked quickly over a grill or in a pan.
- Braising and Stewing: Veal was simmered gently in flavorful liquids to enhance tenderness and flavor.
- Marinating: Veal was marinated to infuse flavor and tenderize the meat before cooking.

The preparation of vitella in ancient Rome showcased the Romans' culinary skills and appreciation for using quality ingredients and techniques to create delicious and diverse veal dishes. Recreating these ancient-inspired veal recipes provides a fascinating glimpse into the rich culinary heritage of ancient Roman cuisine. Adjust the ingredients and cooking methods based on historical references and modern interpretations to enjoy the flavors of vitella in your own kitchen.

Jowles of Sturgeon: Sturgeon cheeks cooked with herbs and spices.

Ingredients for Jowles of Sturgeon:

- 1 pound sturgeon cheeks (or substitute with other firm fish cheeks)
- 2 tablespoons olive oil
- 2 garlic cloves, minced
- 1 tablespoon chopped fresh parsley
- 1 tablespoon chopped fresh dill
- Juice of 1 lemon
- Salt and pepper, to taste
- Optional: Red pepper flakes or paprika, for added spice

Instructions:

1. Prepare the Sturgeon Cheeks:
    - Rinse the sturgeon cheeks under cold water and pat them dry with paper towels.
2. Sauté the Cheeks:
    - In a skillet or frying pan, heat the olive oil over medium-high heat.
    - Add the minced garlic to the pan and sauté for about 30 seconds until fragrant.
3. Cook the Sturgeon Cheeks:
    - Carefully place the sturgeon cheeks in the skillet, making sure they are in a single layer.
    - Cook the cheeks for about 3-4 minutes on each side, or until they are lightly browned and cooked through.
4. Season with Herbs and Spices:
    - Sprinkle the chopped fresh parsley and dill over the sturgeon cheeks.
    - Squeeze the lemon juice over the fish.
    - Season with salt, pepper, and optional red pepper flakes or paprika, according to taste.
5. Serve:
    - Transfer the cooked sturgeon cheeks to a serving platter or individual plates.
6. Garnish and Enjoy:
    - Garnish with additional fresh herbs and lemon wedges if desired.
    - Serve the Jowles of Sturgeon as a flavorful and elegant seafood dish.

Tips and Serving Suggestions:

- Side Dishes: Serve the sturgeon cheeks with steamed vegetables, roasted potatoes, or a fresh salad.
- Wine Pairing: Enjoy this seafood dish with a crisp white wine such as Sauvignon Blanc or Chardonnay.
- Variations: Feel free to experiment with different herbs and spices based on your preferences. Consider adding a splash of white wine or fish broth for extra flavor.

Jowles of Sturgeon represents a unique and delicious preparation of fish cheeks in ancient Roman cuisine, showcasing the Romans' appreciation for seafood and culinary craftsmanship. Recreating this dish offers a taste of history and a delightful way to explore the flavors of ancient Rome in a modern kitchen setting. Adjust the ingredients and cooking techniques to suit your taste and enjoy the rich flavors of sturgeon cheeks cooked with herbs and spices.

Epityrum: Olive relish with herbs and vinegar.

Ingredients for Epityrum (Olive Relish):

- 1 cup pitted black or green olives, preferably Kalamata or Castelvetrano
- 2 tablespoons extra virgin olive oil
- 1 tablespoon red wine vinegar or white wine vinegar
- 1 clove garlic, minced
- 1 tablespoon chopped fresh parsley
- 1 tablespoon chopped fresh mint
- 1 teaspoon chopped fresh thyme (or use dried thyme)
- Salt and black pepper, to taste

Instructions:

1. Prepare the Olives:
    - If using whole olives, pit them and chop them into small pieces. Alternatively, you can use pre-pitted olives.
2. Make the Epityrum:
    - In a mixing bowl, combine the chopped olives, minced garlic, chopped herbs (parsley, mint, thyme), extra virgin olive oil, and red wine vinegar.
    - Mix well to combine all the ingredients.
3. Season and Adjust:
    - Taste the Epityrum and season with salt and black pepper according to your preference. Adjust the amount of vinegar and olive oil to achieve the desired consistency and flavor.
4. Chill (Optional):
    - For best flavor, let the Epityrum sit in the refrigerator for at least 30 minutes before serving to allow the flavors to meld together.
5. Serve:
    - Transfer the Epityrum to a serving bowl or dish.
    - Serve as a condiment or relish alongside bread, crackers, cheese, grilled vegetables, or as a topping for salads and sandwiches.

Variations and Tips:

- Herb Variations: Feel free to experiment with different fresh herbs such as basil, rosemary, or oregano to customize the flavor of your Epityrum.
- Additional Ingredients: Add chopped capers, sun-dried tomatoes, or lemon zest for extra flavor and texture.

- Spice it Up: For a spicy version, add a pinch of red pepper flakes or a dash of hot sauce.

Epityrum is a versatile and flavorful olive relish that adds a Mediterranean touch to your meals. Enjoy this ancient-inspired condiment as a delicious accompaniment to various dishes or as a tasty appetizer spread. The combination of olives, herbs, and vinegar creates a delightful burst of flavors that will transport you to the culinary traditions of ancient Rome. Adjust the ingredients and seasoning to suit your taste preferences and culinary creations!

Frisi Apiciani: Fried fish or seafood.

Ingredients for Frisi Apiciani (Fried Fish or Seafood):

- 1 pound fresh fish fillets (such as cod, haddock, or sole) or seafood (such as shrimp, calamari, or scallops)
- 1 cup all-purpose flour
- Salt and pepper, to taste
- 2 eggs, beaten
- 1 cup breadcrumbs (or use finely ground stale bread)
- Olive oil or vegetable oil, for frying
- Lemon wedges, for serving

Instructions:

1. Prepare the Fish or Seafood:
    - If using fish fillets, cut them into manageable pieces. If using seafood like shrimp or calamari, clean and prepare them as needed.
2. Set Up Dredging Station:
    - In separate shallow bowls or plates, prepare three stations: one with flour seasoned with salt and pepper, one with beaten eggs, and one with breadcrumbs.
3. Dredge the Fish or Seafood:
    - Dredge each piece of fish or seafood in the seasoned flour, shaking off any excess.
    - Dip the floured fish or seafood into the beaten eggs, ensuring it's coated all over.
    - Finally, coat the fish or seafood in the breadcrumbs, pressing gently to adhere.
4. Heat the Oil:
    - In a large skillet or frying pan, heat enough olive oil or vegetable oil to cover the bottom of the pan (about 1/2 inch deep) over medium-high heat until hot but not smoking.
5. Fry the Fish or Seafood:
    - Carefully place the coated fish or seafood pieces into the hot oil in a single layer, without overcrowding the pan. Fry in batches if necessary.
    - Fry the fish or seafood for 2-3 minutes on each side, or until golden brown and cooked through. Cooking time will vary depending on the thickness of the pieces.
6. Drain and Serve:

- Use a slotted spoon or tongs to transfer the fried fish or seafood to a plate lined with paper towels to drain excess oil.
- Serve the Frisi Apiciani hot, garnished with lemon wedges for squeezing over the crispy fried pieces.

Serving Suggestions:

- Side Dishes: Serve Frisi Apiciani with a side of fresh salad, roasted vegetables, or crispy fries.
- Sauces: Offer dipping sauces such as tartar sauce, aioli, or marinara sauce for added flavor.

Frisi Apiciani is a delightful dish that reflects the ancient Roman tradition of preparing fish and seafood in a simple yet flavorful manner. Recreate this ancient-inspired fried dish to experience a taste of history and the culinary influence of Apicius on Roman cuisine. Adjust the ingredients and seasonings to suit your preferences and enjoy this crispy and satisfying seafood dish with family and friends!

Fritillus: Fried pastries served with honey or sweet sauces.

Ingredients for Fritillus (Fried Pastries):

- 1 cup all-purpose flour
- 1/4 teaspoon salt
- 1 tablespoon sugar
- 1/2 teaspoon ground cinnamon (optional)
- 1 large egg
- 1/4 cup milk
- Vegetable oil, for frying
- Honey or sweet sauce (e.g., date syrup, grape syrup) for drizzling

Instructions:

1. Prepare the Dough:
    - In a mixing bowl, combine the flour, salt, sugar, and ground cinnamon (if using).
    - In a separate bowl, whisk together the egg and milk.
    - Gradually add the egg mixture to the dry ingredients, stirring until a smooth dough forms. Add more flour if needed to achieve a workable dough consistency.
2. Shape the Fritillus:
    - On a lightly floured surface, roll out the dough into a thin sheet (about 1/4 inch thick).
    - Use a knife or pizza cutter to cut the dough into small rectangles or diamond shapes, or use cookie cutters to create desired shapes.
3. Fry the Pastries:
    - In a deep skillet or pot, heat vegetable oil over medium-high heat until hot (about 350°F or 175°C).
    - Carefully add a few pieces of dough at a time to the hot oil, frying in batches to avoid overcrowding.
    - Fry the fritillus for 1-2 minutes on each side, or until golden brown and crispy. Use a slotted spoon to transfer them to a plate lined with paper towels to drain excess oil.
4. Serve:
    - Arrange the fried fritillus on a serving platter.
    - Drizzle honey or sweet sauce generously over the warm pastries.
5. Enjoy:

- Serve the fritillus immediately while still warm and crispy, enjoying the delightful combination of fried dough and sweet honey or sauce.

Variations and Tips:

- Flavor Enhancements: Experiment with different flavorings such as orange zest, vanilla extract, or nutmeg in the dough for added complexity.
- Toppings: In addition to honey or sweet sauces, sprinkle powdered sugar or ground nuts over the fritillus for extra texture and flavor.
- Storage: Fritillus are best enjoyed fresh and warm, but you can store leftovers in an airtight container at room temperature for up to a day and reheat briefly in the oven to crisp them up before serving.

Fritillus provides a delightful taste of ancient Roman cuisine, showcasing the simplicity and deliciousness of fried pastries paired with sweet toppings. Recreate this ancient-inspired dessert at home to experience a historical treat that's sure to satisfy your sweet tooth! Adjust the recipe to suit your preferences and enjoy the crispy, honey-drizzled goodness of fritillus with family and friends.

Aliter Dulcia: Assorted sweet dishes and desserts.

Examples of Aliter Dulcia (Assorted Sweet Dishes):

1. Patina de Piris (Pear Custard): A baked custard made with ripe pears, eggs, honey, and spices like cinnamon or nutmeg.
2. Gustum de Prunis (Plum Dessert): Stewed plums sweetened with honey or fruit syrup, flavored with aromatic herbs like mint or bay leaves.
3. Libum (Cheesecake): A sweet cake made with flour, cheese (such as ricotta), eggs, and honey, often flavored with bay leaves.
4. Gustum de Nuce (Walnut Sweetmeat): Candied walnuts or a sweet nut paste flavored with honey, spices, and sometimes wine.
5. Gustum de Melimelum (Honeyed Apples): Baked or poached apples coated in honey and sprinkled with nuts or spices.
6. Gustum de Cerebellis (Spelt and Honey Dessert): A dish made with spelt (farro) grains cooked in honey and flavored with herbs or spices.

Ingredients Used in Aliter Dulcia:

- Honey: A primary sweetener used in ancient Roman desserts.
- Fruits: Including pears, apples, plums, figs, and dates, often used fresh or dried.
- Nuts: Such as almonds, walnuts, and pine nuts, adding texture and flavor to sweet dishes.
- Spices: Commonly used spices like cinnamon, nutmeg, cloves, and pepper to enhance flavor.
- Cheese: Ricotta or other soft cheeses were used in some sweet preparations like Libum.

Cooking Techniques for Aliter Dulcia:

- Baking: Many sweet dishes were baked in ovens or clay pots.
- Stewing: Fruits and nuts were often stewed or poached in sweet syrups.
- Frying: Some desserts may have involved frying or pan-cooking, similar to modern fritters.

Enjoying Aliter Dulcia Today:

You can recreate the spirit of Aliter Dulcia by experimenting with ancient

Roman-inspired sweet recipes using traditional ingredients and techniques. Combine

honey, fruits, nuts, and spices to create indulgent and flavorful desserts that pay homage to the rich culinary heritage of ancient Rome. Customize the recipes based on historical references and your own taste preferences to enjoy a taste of ancient Roman sweets!

Alicam: Barley or wheat porridge served with honey.

Ingredients for Alicam (Barley or Wheat Porridge with Honey):

- 1 cup pearl barley or cracked wheat (farro)
- 4 cups water
- Pinch of salt
- Honey, to taste (about 2-3 tablespoons per serving)
- Ground cinnamon or nutmeg, for garnish (optional)

Instructions:

1. Prepare the Barley or Wheat:
    - Rinse the pearl barley or cracked wheat under cold water.
    - In a saucepan, combine the barley or wheat with 4 cups of water and a pinch of salt.
2. Cook the Porridge:
    - Bring the water to a boil over medium-high heat.
    - Reduce the heat to low, cover the saucepan, and simmer the barley or wheat for about 30-40 minutes, or until tender and cooked through. Stir occasionally.
3. Serve with Honey:
    - Once the barley or wheat is cooked to your desired consistency (it should be soft and creamy), remove the saucepan from the heat.
    - Spoon the cooked barley or wheat into serving bowls.
4. Sweeten with Honey:
    - Drizzle honey generously over each serving of the warm barley or wheat porridge, according to taste.
5. Garnish:
    - Optionally, sprinkle ground cinnamon or nutmeg over the porridge for added flavor and aroma.
6. Enjoy:
    - Serve the Alicam immediately while warm, allowing the honey to melt into the porridge and create a deliciously sweet and satisfying dish.

Variations and Tips:

- Dried Fruits: Add chopped dried fruits such as raisins, dates, or figs to the porridge during cooking for extra sweetness and texture.

- Nuts: Garnish the Alicam with toasted nuts like almonds or walnuts for crunch and flavor.
- Spices: Experiment with different spices like cardamom, cloves, or ginger to enhance the flavor of the porridge.
- Milk: For a creamier texture, you can use milk instead of water to cook the barley or wheat, then drizzle with honey before serving.

Alicam represents a humble yet delicious dish from ancient Rome, showcasing the use of basic ingredients like barley or wheat and honey to create a comforting and sweet porridge. Recreate this ancient-inspired recipe at home to experience a taste of history and enjoy a warm and nourishing breakfast or dessert. Adjust the ingredients and sweeteners based on your preferences to make this dish your own while honoring the culinary traditions of ancient Roman cuisine.

Mulsum: Honey-sweetened wine or mead.

Ingredients for Mulsum (Honey-Sweetened Wine):

- 1 bottle (750 ml) of red wine or white wine (choose a medium-bodied wine)
- 1/2 cup honey (adjust to taste)
- Optional: Whole spices such as cinnamon sticks, cloves, or bay leaves

Instructions:

1. Prepare the Mulsum Mixture:
    - In a small saucepan, combine the honey with a splash of water (about 1/4 cup) over low heat.
    - Heat gently, stirring occasionally, until the honey is dissolved completely into a smooth syrup. Avoid boiling.
2. Infuse the Wine with Honey:
    - In a large pitcher or decanter, pour the entire bottle of wine.
    - Slowly pour the warm honey syrup into the wine, stirring gently to combine.
3. Optional Spices:
    - If desired, add whole spices such as cinnamon sticks, cloves, or bay leaves to the Mulsum mixture for additional flavor. Let the spices infuse for at least 30 minutes.
4. Chill (Optional):
    - Place the Mulsum in the refrigerator to chill for at least 1 hour before serving, allowing the flavors to meld together.
5. Serve and Enjoy:
    - Pour the Mulsum into glasses or cups.
    - Garnish with a cinnamon stick or a slice of orange if desired.
    - Serve Mulsum chilled or at room temperature as a delightful and festive drink.

Variations and Tips:

- Wine Selection: Choose a wine that you enjoy drinking, such as a red wine (like a Merlot or Syrah) or a white wine (like a Chardonnay or Riesling). The sweetness of the honey will complement the wine's flavor.
- Honey Flavor: Experiment with different types of honey for varying flavors. For a more pronounced honey flavor, use a bold or floral honey variety.

- Spice Variations: Customize the Mulsum by adding other spices like star anise, cardamom pods, or grated nutmeg to create your own unique blend.
- Mead Option: Instead of wine, you can use mead (honey wine) as the base for Mulsum, further enhancing the honeyed character of the drink.

Mulsum is a delightful and historic beverage that captures the essence of ancient Roman hospitality and culinary tradition. Enjoy this honey-sweetened wine with friends and family, celebrating the flavors of antiquity while savoring a taste of Roman culture. Adjust the sweetness and spices to suit your preferences and raise a glass of Mulsum to Roman ingenuity and the simple pleasures of honey-infused libations.

Laserpitium: Aromatic herb used in cooking.

Laserpitium in Ancient Roman Cuisine:

1. Flavor Profile: Laserpitium was described as having a bold, aromatic flavor similar to fennel, lovage, or even asafoetida. It was known for its pungent and slightly bitter taste.
2. Culinary Uses: Laserpitium was used as a seasoning or flavoring agent in cooking, adding depth and complexity to various dishes.
3. Medicinal Properties: In addition to its culinary applications, laserpitium was also valued for its medicinal properties in ancient times, believed to have digestive and therapeutic benefits.

Hypothetical Laserpitium Usage in Recipes:

While we cannot replicate laserpitium precisely today due to its extinction, we can imagine how it might have been used in ancient Roman recipes based on historical records and flavor profiles similar to other herbs:

- Laserpitium Flavored Sauces: Laserpitium might have been used to flavor sauces and dressings for meat or vegetable dishes, adding a unique herbal note.
- Herb-Rubbed Meats: Laserpitium could have been part of herb rubs or marinades for meats such as lamb or poultry, enhancing the overall flavor profile.
- Herbal Seasoning: Laserpitium could have been incorporated into soups, stews, or savory pies for added depth of flavor.

Modern Substitutes for Laserpitium:

To replicate the flavor profile of laserpitium in modern cooking, you can experiment with the following herbs and spices known for their similarities:

- Fennel: Fresh or dried fennel fronds or seeds can provide a similar aromatic and slightly sweet flavor.
- Lovage: Lovage leaves or seeds have a flavor reminiscent of celery and can contribute a robust herbal note to dishes.
- Asafoetida: Known for its pungent aroma, a small amount of asafoetida (also called "devil's dung") can add depth and umami to dishes, though it should be used sparingly.

Experiment with these herbs and spices to capture the essence of laserpitium and explore the ancient Roman culinary world through modern interpretations. While laserpitium itself is lost to history, its legacy lives on in the quest to rediscover and appreciate the diverse flavors of antiquity.

Cibarium: General term for food or meals.

Understanding Cibarium in Ancient Roman Context:

1. Meaning: The word "cibarium" comes from the Latin root "cibus," which simply means "food." It represents the basic sustenance needed for survival and daily nourishment.
2. Usage: In ancient Roman society, "cibarium" was a broad term that encompassed various aspects of food and eating, including:
    - Ingredients used in cooking and meal preparation.
    - Prepared dishes and culinary creations.
    - The act of dining and communal eating experiences.
    - The overall culture and traditions surrounding food consumption.
3. Cibarium in Daily Life: The concept of cibarium was central to daily life in ancient Rome, reflecting the importance of food in social, cultural, and economic contexts. Meals were not only about satisfying hunger but also about socializing, celebrating, and showcasing culinary skills.

Implications of Cibarium in Roman Cuisine:

- Diverse Ingredients: Cibarium included a wide range of ingredients commonly used in Roman cooking, such as grains (like wheat and barley), vegetables, fruits, meats (including poultry, pork, and game), fish, dairy products, and various herbs and spices.
- Meal Preparation: Roman cooks and chefs (called "coqui" or "archimagiri") played a vital role in transforming raw ingredients into flavorful dishes served during meals.
- Eating Customs: Meals in ancient Rome often consisted of multiple courses (mensae primae, secundae, etc.), showcasing a variety of flavors and textures. Dining etiquette and social hierarchy were also important aspects of Roman meal culture.

Modern Interpretation of Cibarium:

Today, the term "cibarium" can evoke a sense of historical culinary heritage and inspire a deeper appreciation for ancient Roman cuisine. Exploring Roman recipes and cooking techniques can offer insights into the diverse and flavorful world of cibarium, highlighting the timeless appeal of food as a universal human experience.

In summary, cibarium represents more than just food—it embodies the essence of sustenance, creativity, and communal enjoyment in ancient Roman culture. Through the lens of cibarium, we can glimpse into the culinary traditions and culinary philosophy that shaped daily life in ancient Rome, leaving a lasting impact on the evolution of gastronomy and dining practices.

Gustum de Pineis: Pine nut desserts and dishes.

Examples of Gustum de Pineis (Pine Nut Dishes):

1. Pine Nut Cakes or Pastries: Ancient Romans likely used pine nuts in cakes, pastries, or sweet breads, either as a garnish or incorporated into the dough for added texture and flavor.
2. Honeyed Pine Nuts: Pine nuts could have been toasted and coated with honey to create a sweet and crunchy treat, similar to modern-day candied nuts.
3. Pine Nut Puddings: Pine nuts might have been mixed into creamy desserts or custards to provide a delightful contrast in texture.
4. Pine Nut Sauces: Ground pine nuts could have been used to thicken and flavor sauces for savory dishes, adding a nutty richness.
5. Pine Nut Stuffings: Pine nuts could have been used as part of stuffings for meats or vegetables, contributing a savory and nutty element.

Recipe Ideas for Gustum de Pineis:

Honeyed Pine Nuts

- Ingredients:
    1. 1 cup pine nuts
    2. 2 tablespoons honey
    3. Pinch of salt
- Instructions:
    1. In a dry skillet over medium heat, toast the pine nuts until golden and fragrant, stirring frequently to prevent burning.
    2. Remove the toasted pine nuts from the skillet and place them in a bowl.
    3. Drizzle honey over the pine nuts while they are still warm, tossing to coat evenly.
    4. Sprinkle a pinch of salt over the honeyed pine nuts for balance.
    5. Let the mixture cool and harden before serving as a sweet and crunchy snack or dessert topping.

Pine Nut and Honey Cake

- Ingredients:
    1. 1 cup all-purpose flour
    2. 1 teaspoon baking powder
    3. 1/2 cup pine nuts, toasted
    4. 1/2 cup honey

5. 1/2 cup unsalted butter, softened
   6. 1/2 cup granulated sugar
   7. 2 large eggs
   8. 1 teaspoon vanilla extract
   9. Pinch of salt
- Instructions:
   1. Preheat the oven to 350°F (175°C) and grease a cake pan.
   2. In a bowl, whisk together the flour, baking powder, and salt.
   3. In another bowl, cream together the softened butter and sugar until light and fluffy.
   4. Beat in the eggs one at a time, then stir in the vanilla extract.
   5. Gradually add the dry ingredients to the wet mixture, mixing until just combined.
   6. Fold in the toasted pine nuts.
   7. Pour the batter into the greased cake pan and bake for 25-30 minutes, or until a toothpick inserted into the center comes out clean.
   8. While the cake is still warm, drizzle honey over the top for added sweetness and flavor.
   9. Let the cake cool before slicing and serving.

Enjoying Gustum de Pineis Today:

Exploring Gustum de Pineis allows us to appreciate the versatility of pine nuts and their role in ancient Roman cuisine. Whether enjoyed in sweet desserts or savory dishes, pine nuts add a distinctive nutty flavor and texture that can be savored in modern interpretations of historical recipes. Experiment with these ideas and incorporate pine nuts into your culinary creations to experience a taste of ancient Rome's flavorful heritage! Adjust the recipes to suit your preferences and celebrate the timeless appeal of pine nuts in gastronomy.

Alicam Cerebellatum: Spelt porridge sweetened with honey.

Ingredients for Alicam Cerebellatum (Spelt Porridge with Honey):

- 1 cup spelt grains (pearled spelt or whole spelt berries)
- 3 cups water
- Pinch of salt
- Honey, to taste (about 2-3 tablespoons)
- Ground cinnamon or nutmeg, for garnish (optional)

Instructions:

1. Prepare the Spelt:
    - Rinse the spelt grains under cold water.
    - In a saucepan, combine the rinsed spelt grains with 3 cups of water and a pinch of salt.
2. Cook the Spelt:
    - Bring the water to a boil over medium-high heat.
    - Reduce the heat to low, cover the saucepan, and simmer the spelt for about 45-60 minutes, or until the grains are tender and have absorbed most of the water. Stir occasionally.
3. Sweeten with Honey:
    - Once the spelt is cooked to your desired consistency (it should be soft and creamy), remove the saucepan from the heat.
    - Stir in honey to taste, starting with about 2 tablespoons and adjusting according to your sweetness preference.
4. Serve:
    - Spoon the sweetened spelt porridge into serving bowls.
    - Optionally, sprinkle ground cinnamon or nutmeg over the porridge for added flavor and aroma.
5. Enjoy:
    - Serve Alicam Cerebellatum warm as a comforting breakfast or dessert, savoring the combination of nutty spelt and natural sweetness from the honey.

Variations and Tips:

- Spice Infusion: Enhance the flavor of Alicam Cerebellatum by infusing the cooking water with a cinnamon stick or a few cloves while simmering the spelt.

- Additions: Consider incorporating chopped nuts (such as almonds or walnuts) or dried fruits (like raisins or chopped dates) into the porridge for extra texture and flavor.
- Milk Option: For a creamier porridge, substitute part of the water with milk (dairy or plant-based) during cooking.

Alicam Cerebellatum offers a glimpse into the ancient Roman diet, highlighting the use of spelt and honey as nutritious and delightful ingredients. Recreate this historical dish at home to experience the simplicity and wholesomeness of ancient Roman cuisine. Customize the recipe with your favorite spices and toppings to make Alicam Cerebellatum a comforting and satisfying meal that pays homage to the culinary traditions of antiquity.

Gustum de Persicis: Peach-based desserts.

Ancient Roman-Inspired Peach Dessert Ideas:

1. Honeyed Peaches:
   - Ingredients: Ripe peaches, honey, ground cinnamon.
   - Instructions: Slice fresh peaches and arrange them in a serving dish. Drizzle with honey and sprinkle with ground cinnamon for a sweet and aromatic treat.
2. Peach and Nut Pudding:
   - Ingredients: Fresh peaches, ground nuts (such as almonds or walnuts), honey, spices (like cinnamon or nutmeg), eggs.
   - Instructions: Prepare a custard-like pudding by blending ground nuts with honey, spices, and beaten eggs. Fold in sliced peaches and bake until set for a deliciously nutty and fruity dessert.
3. Peach Fritters:
   - Ingredients: Ripe peaches, batter (made with flour, eggs, milk), honey for drizzling.
   - Instructions: Dip peach slices or halves in a simple batter and fry until golden brown. Serve hot with a drizzle of honey for a crispy and sweet treat.
4. Peach and Wine Compote:
   - Ingredients: Peeled and sliced peaches, sweet white wine, honey, fresh mint leaves.
   - Instructions: Simmer sliced peaches in sweet white wine and honey until tender. Serve chilled or at room temperature, garnished with fresh mint leaves.
5. Peach Tarts or Pastries:
   - Ingredients: Prepared pastry dough, sliced peaches, honey or sugar for sweetening.
   - Instructions: Arrange sliced peaches on pastry dough, fold over the edges, and bake until golden. Drizzle with honey or sprinkle with sugar before serving for a delightful peach pastry.

Tips for Creating Gustum de Persicis:

- Choose Ripe Peaches: Use ripe and flavorful peaches for the best results, as they will provide natural sweetness and juiciness to the desserts.
- Balance Sweetness: Adjust the sweetness of the desserts by using honey, sugar, or other natural sweeteners according to your taste preference.

- Incorporate Spices: Enhance the flavor profile of peach-based desserts with spices like cinnamon, nutmeg, or cloves for a warm and aromatic touch.
- Experiment with Presentation: Get creative with serving and garnishing your Gustum de Persicis creations to make them visually appealing and inviting.

By drawing inspiration from historical ingredients and flavors, you can recreate Gustum de Persicis in a modern kitchen, celebrating the delightful combination of peaches with honey and spices. Experiment with these ideas and adapt them to your own culinary style to experience a taste of ancient Roman peach-based desserts that are both delicious and evocative of antiquity.

Tyropatinam: Cheesecake-like desserts.

Ancient Roman-Inspired Tyropatinam Recipe:

Ingredients:

- 1 cup ricotta cheese or fresh soft cheese (such as goat cheese or farmer's cheese)
- 2 large eggs
- 1/4 cup honey (plus extra for drizzling)
- 1 teaspoon ground cinnamon
- Zest of 1 lemon (optional)
- Pinch of salt
- Olive oil or melted butter, for greasing

Instructions:

1. Preheat the Oven: Preheat your oven to 350°F (175°C). Grease a small baking dish or pie dish with olive oil or melted butter.
2. Prepare the Cheesecake Batter:
    - In a mixing bowl, combine the ricotta cheese, eggs, honey, ground cinnamon, lemon zest (if using), and a pinch of salt. Use a whisk or hand mixer to blend everything together until smooth and well combined.
3. Bake the Tyropatinam:
    - Pour the cheesecake batter into the prepared baking dish, spreading it out evenly.
    - Place the dish in the preheated oven and bake for about 25-30 minutes, or until the edges are set and lightly golden, and the center is firm but slightly jiggly.
4. Cool and Serve:
    - Remove the Tyropatinam from the oven and let it cool to room temperature.
    - Once cooled, drizzle additional honey over the top for sweetness.
    - Cut into slices and serve as a delicious and creamy cheesecake-like dessert with ancient Roman flair.

Tips for Making Tyropatinam:

- Cheese Selection: Use ricotta cheese for a mild and creamy texture, or experiment with other fresh soft cheeses based on availability and preference.

- Sweetening: Adjust the amount of honey according to your desired level of sweetness. Ancient Roman desserts often featured honey as a primary sweetener.
- Flavor Variations: Customize the flavor of Tyropatinam by adding spices like nutmeg, cloves, or cardamom for additional complexity.

Enjoying Tyropatinam Today:

Tyropatinam offers a delightful taste of ancient Roman cheesecake-like desserts, showcasing the simplicity and elegance of Roman culinary traditions. Serve this creamy and subtly sweet treat as a dessert or snack, and savor the historical flavors that transport you to ancient Rome. Experiment with the recipe and make it your own while appreciating the timeless appeal of cheesecake in Roman gastronomy.

Gustum de Piris: Pear-based dishes and desserts.

Ancient Roman-Inspired Pear Dessert Ideas:

1. Honey-Roasted Pears:
    - Ingredients: Ripe pears, honey, ground cinnamon or cloves, butter.
    - Instructions: Halve and core the pears, then place them in a baking dish. Drizzle with honey, sprinkle with ground cinnamon or cloves, and dot with butter. Roast in the oven until tender and caramelized.
2. Pear and Walnut Salad:
    - Ingredients: Sliced pears, toasted walnuts, arugula or mixed greens, olive oil, vinegar, honey.
    - Instructions: Toss sliced pears and toasted walnuts with fresh greens. Dress with a vinaigrette made of olive oil, vinegar, and honey for a refreshing salad.
3. Poached Pears in Spiced Wine:
    - Ingredients: Whole pears, red wine, honey, spices (such as cinnamon sticks, cloves, and star anise).
    - Instructions: Peel the pears and poach them in a mixture of red wine sweetened with honey and infused with spices until tender and infused with flavor.
4. Pear Custard Tart:
    - Ingredients: Prepared pastry dough, sliced pears, custard (made with eggs, milk or cream, sugar), honey.
    - Instructions: Arrange sliced pears on pastry dough and pour custard over them. Bake until the custard is set and the crust is golden. Drizzle with honey before serving.

Gustum De Piris

Honey-Roasted Pears with Cinnamon

Ingredients:

- 4 ripe pears, halved and cored
- 2-3 tablespoons honey
- 1/2 teaspoon ground cinnamon
- 2 tablespoons unsalted butter, cut into small pieces

Instructions:

1. Preheat the Oven: Preheat your oven to 375°F (190°C).
2. Prepare the Pears: Place the halved and cored pears in a baking dish, cut side up.
3. Drizzle with Honey and Spices: Drizzle the pears with honey, making sure to coat each pear evenly. Sprinkle ground cinnamon over the pears.
4. Add Butter: Dot the pears with small pieces of butter.
5. Roast the Pears: Place the baking dish in the preheated oven and roast for about 25-30 minutes, or until the pears are tender and caramelized, basting occasionally with the honey-butter mixture.
6. Serve: Remove the roasted pears from the oven. Serve warm as a delightful and simple pear dessert, drizzling any remaining honey-butter sauce over the pears before serving.

Tips for Enjoying Gustum de Piris:

- Pear Selection: Choose ripe but firm pears for cooking and baking to ensure they hold their shape during preparation.
- Sweetness Level: Adjust the amount of honey used based on the natural sweetness of the pears and your personal preference.
- Spice Variations: Experiment with different spices like cloves, nutmeg, or cardamom to complement the flavor of the pears.

Gustum de Piris offers a glimpse into the delicious ways ancient Romans enjoyed pears in their cuisine. By incorporating these ideas and recipes into your culinary repertoire, you can experience the timeless appeal of pear-based dishes and desserts that celebrate the bounty of nature and the flavors of antiquity.

Pisum: Pea dishes prepared with various ingredients.

Ancient Roman-Inspired Pea Dish Ideas:

1. Pea and Mint Soup:
    - Ingredients: Fresh or frozen peas, vegetable broth, fresh mint leaves, onion, garlic, olive oil.
    - Instructions: Sauté diced onion and minced garlic in olive oil until soft. Add peas and vegetable broth, then simmer until peas are tender. Blend the soup until smooth, then stir in chopped fresh mint leaves before serving.
2. Peas with Pancetta and Onions:
    - Ingredients: Peas, diced pancetta (or bacon), diced onion, olive oil, salt, black pepper.
    - Instructions: Sauté diced pancetta in olive oil until crispy. Add diced onion and cook until softened. Add peas and cook until heated through. Season with salt and black pepper before serving.
3. Pea and Cheese Risotto:
    - Ingredients: Arborio rice, peas, grated Parmesan cheese, vegetable broth, onion, white wine, butter.
    - Instructions: Sauté diced onion in butter until translucent. Add Arborio rice and cook until lightly toasted. Deglaze with white wine, then gradually add vegetable broth while stirring constantly. Stir in peas and grated Parmesan cheese just before serving.
4. Peas with Mint and Honey:
    - Ingredients: Peas, fresh mint leaves, honey, butter, salt.
    - Instructions: Cook peas until tender, then toss with chopped fresh mint leaves, a drizzle of honey, and a knob of butter. Season with salt to taste before serving.

Pisum with Pancetta and Onions

Ingredients:

- 2 cups fresh or frozen peas
- 100g diced pancetta (or bacon)
- 1 small onion, diced
- 2 tablespoons olive oil
- Salt and black pepper, to taste

Instructions:

1. Cook Pancetta: In a skillet or frying pan, heat olive oil over medium heat. Add diced pancetta and cook until crispy.
2. Sauté Onions: Add diced onion to the skillet with the pancetta. Sauté until the onions are soft and translucent.
3. Add Peas: Add fresh or frozen peas to the skillet with the cooked pancetta and onions. Stir well to combine.
4. Season and Serve: Season the peas with salt and black pepper, adjusting to taste. Cook for a few more minutes until the peas are heated through.
5. Serve: Transfer the Pisum (peas with pancetta and onions) to a serving dish. Serve hot as a delicious and flavorful side dish or light main course.

Tips for Enjoying Pisum:

- Fresh vs. Frozen Peas: Use fresh peas when in season for the best flavor and texture. Frozen peas are a convenient option and work well in cooked dishes.
- Seasoning: Peas pair well with savory ingredients like pancetta, onions, garlic, and herbs. Experiment with different flavor combinations to suit your taste preferences.
- Ancient Roman Influence: Imagine the flavors and techniques used in ancient Roman cooking while preparing Pisum, appreciating the simplicity and elegance of peas in historical culinary traditions.

Pisum offers a delightful way to incorporate peas into your cooking, inspired by ancient Roman cuisine. By exploring these ideas and recipes, you can experience the timeless appeal of peas as a versatile and delicious ingredient in savory dishes that celebrate the culinary heritage of antiquity.

Patina Apiciana: Baked dishes named after Apicius.

Roman-Inspired Baked Dish Recipe:

Ingredients:

- 6 eggs
- 1 cup cooked chicken, diced
- 1 cup cooked mushrooms, sliced
- 1 leek, thinly sliced
- 1/2 cup grated hard cheese (such as Pecorino Romano or Parmesan)
- 2 tablespoons fresh parsley, chopped
- 1 teaspoon ground black pepper
- 1/2 teaspoon fish sauce (or soy sauce as a substitute)
- 1 tablespoon olive oil
- Butter or olive oil, for greasing

Instructions:

1. Preheat the Oven: Preheat your oven to 350°F (175°C). Grease a baking dish with butter or olive oil.
2. Prepare the Ingredients: In a bowl, whisk together the eggs. Add diced chicken, sliced mushrooms, leek, grated cheese, chopped parsley, black pepper, and fish sauce. Mix well to combine.
3. Bake the Dish: Pour the egg mixture into the greased baking dish. Place in the preheated oven and bake for 25-30 minutes, or until the top is golden brown and the center is set.
4. Serve: Remove the baked dish from the oven and let it cool slightly before slicing and serving. Enjoy as a flavorful and satisfying main course or side dish inspired by Patina Apiciana.

Tips for Making a Roman Baked Dish:

- Ingredient Substitutions: Feel free to substitute ingredients based on availability and personal preference while staying true to the general style and flavors of ancient Roman cuisine.
- Experiment with Flavors: Explore Roman spices and seasonings like lovage, dill, or wine vinegar to enhance the authenticity of your baked dish.
- Presentation: Garnish your baked dish with fresh herbs or a sprinkle of grated cheese before serving for an attractive presentation.

By embracing the spirit of Patina Apiciana and ancient Roman culinary traditions, you can create a delicious and historically inspired baked dish that celebrates the rich heritage of Roman gastronomy. Adjust the recipe to suit your taste and enjoy a taste of ancient Rome in your modern kitchen!

Gustum de Nuce: Walnut-based dishes and desserts.

Ancient Roman-Inspired Walnut Dish Ideas:

1. Walnut and Honey Tart:
    - Ingredients: Prepared pastry dough, chopped walnuts, honey, eggs, sugar.
    - Instructions: Line a tart pan with pastry dough. Fill with a mixture of chopped walnuts, honey, beaten eggs, and sugar. Bake until set and golden for a delightful walnut tart.
2. Walnut and Cheese Salad:
    - Ingredients: Mixed greens, crumbled cheese (such as feta or goat cheese), chopped walnuts, olive oil, vinegar, honey.
    - Instructions: Toss mixed greens with crumbled cheese, chopped walnuts, olive oil, vinegar, and a drizzle of honey for a savory-sweet salad.
3. Stuffed Dates with Walnuts:
    - Ingredients: Medjool dates, walnuts, honey.
    - Instructions: Remove pits from dates and stuff each date with a walnut half. Drizzle with honey for a quick and satisfying snack or dessert.
4. Walnut and Raisin Bread:
    - Ingredients: Bread dough, chopped walnuts, raisins.
    - Instructions: Knead chopped walnuts and raisins into bread dough before baking for a hearty and flavorful loaf.

Walnut and Honey Pastry

Ingredients:

- 1 sheet of puff pastry (or homemade pastry dough)
- 1 cup chopped walnuts
- 1/4 cup honey
- 1 egg, beaten (for egg wash)
- Powdered sugar, for dusting (optional)

Instructions:

1. Preheat the Oven: Preheat your oven to 375°F (190°C). Line a baking sheet with parchment paper.
2. Prepare the Pastry: Roll out the puff pastry sheet into a rectangle on a lightly floured surface. Transfer the pastry to the prepared baking sheet.
3. Make the Walnut Filling: In a bowl, mix together the chopped walnuts and honey until well combined.
4. Assemble the Pastry:
    - Spread the walnut and honey mixture evenly over the pastry sheet, leaving a border around the edges.
    - Fold the edges of the pastry inward to create a rustic tart crust.
5. Brush with Egg Wash: Brush the edges of the pastry with beaten egg for a golden finish.
6. Bake the Pastry: Place the pastry in the preheated oven and bake for 20-25 minutes, or until the pastry is puffed and golden brown.
7. Serve: Remove the walnut and honey pastry from the oven and let it cool slightly. Dust with powdered sugar if desired. Slice and serve warm as a delicious Gustum de Nuce-inspired dessert.

Tips for Enjoying Gustum de Nuce:

- Quality Walnuts: Use fresh and high-quality walnuts for the best flavor and texture in your dishes and desserts.
- Experiment with Combinations: Pair walnuts with other ingredients like honey, cheese, fruits, or spices to create unique flavor profiles.
- Explore Roman Flavors: Incorporate Roman-inspired spices or flavorings like cinnamon, nutmeg, or wine vinegar to enhance the authenticity of your walnut-based dishes.

By embracing the versatility of walnuts and exploring ancient Roman culinary influences, you can create Gustum de Nuce-inspired dishes and desserts that celebrate the rich heritage of Roman gastronomy. Customize the recipes to suit your taste preferences and enjoy the delightful flavors of walnuts in both savory and sweet creations!

Panis: Bread, a staple of Roman cuisine.

Types of Roman Bread:

1. Panis Quadratus (Square Bread):
   - This was a common type of bread in ancient Rome, typically made with wheat flour, water, salt, and sometimes yeast or sourdough starter. Panis quadratus was a simple, flat bread baked in square or rectangular shapes.
2. Panis Articus (Artisan Bread):
   - Artisanal breads were crafted by skilled bakers using high-quality flour and often enriched with ingredients like olive oil, honey, or herbs. These breads were favored by the wealthy and served at banquets.
3. Panis Secundarius (Secondary Bread):
   - This referred to a variety of breads that were softer and lighter than panis quadratus, often enjoyed as a secondary bread alongside main dishes.
4. Fermented Bread:
   - Roman bakers used natural fermentation processes to leaven bread, resulting in a range of textures and flavors. Some breads were left to rise longer for a more airy texture, while others were denser and more compact.

Ingredients and Techniques:

- Flour: Wheat was the primary grain used for making bread in ancient Rome, although other grains like barley and spelt were also utilized, especially by lower-income households.
- Leavening: Yeast was sometimes used to leaven bread, or bakers relied on natural fermentation from wild yeast cultures present in the environment.
- Baking Methods: Roman bread was baked in communal ovens called furni, which were a vital part of urban life. Bakers produced large quantities of bread daily to meet the demand of the population.

Role of Bread in Roman Meals:

- Main Staple: Bread formed the basis of most Roman meals, serving as a source of sustenance and nourishment.
- Accompaniment: Bread was often paired with other foods such as cheese, olives, vegetables, and meats, creating simple but satisfying meals.
- Symbol of Social Status: The quality and type of bread consumed reflected one's social status, with wealthy Romans enjoying finer, artisanal breads.

Modern Interpretations of Roman Bread:

While specific ancient Roman bread recipes may be scarce, modern bakers and historians have recreated Roman breads using historical techniques and ingredients. By experimenting with ancient grains, natural leavening methods, and traditional baking practices, enthusiasts can experience the taste of panis as it was enjoyed in ancient Rome.

Recreating Roman Bread at Home:

For those interested in baking Roman-style bread at home, consider using whole wheat or spelt flour, experimenting with natural fermentation (sourdough), and exploring Roman flavorings like olive oil, honey, and herbs. By embracing the heritage of panis, you can connect with the culinary traditions of ancient Rome and appreciate the significance of bread in shaping Roman culture and society.

Lenticulae: Lentil dishes prepared in different styles.

Ancient Roman-Inspired Lentil Dish Ideas:

1. Lentil Stew with Vegetables:
    - Ingredients: Lentils, onions, carrots, celery, garlic, olive oil, broth or water, herbs (such as bay leaves, thyme, or parsley), salt, and pepper.
    - Instructions: Sauté diced onions, carrots, celery, and garlic in olive oil until softened. Add lentils and cover with broth or water. Simmer until lentils are tender and flavors are well combined. Season with herbs, salt, and pepper.
2. Lentil and Sausage Casserole:
    - Ingredients: Lentils, Italian sausage (or other sausage of choice), tomatoes, onion, garlic, olive oil, broth or water, red wine vinegar, fresh herbs (such as rosemary or sage), salt, and pepper.
    - Instructions: Brown sliced sausage in olive oil. Add diced onions and garlic, then stir in lentils, tomatoes, and broth or water. Simmer until lentils are cooked and flavors meld together. Finish with a splash of red wine vinegar and chopped fresh herbs.
3. Lentil Salad with Herbs and Lemon Dressing:
    - Ingredients: Cooked lentils, chopped fresh herbs (such as parsley, mint, and dill), lemon juice, olive oil, salt, and pepper.
    - Instructions: Toss cooked lentils with chopped herbs, lemon juice, olive oil, salt, and pepper. Serve as a refreshing and nutritious salad.
4. Spiced Lentil Soup:
    - Ingredients: Lentils, onions, garlic, ginger, spices (such as cumin, coriander, turmeric), coconut milk (optional), broth or water, salt, and pepper.
    - Instructions: Sauté diced onions, garlic, and ginger in olive oil. Add lentils, spices, and broth or water. Simmer until lentils are tender. For a creamy texture, stir in coconut milk before serving.

Lentil Stew with Vegetables

Ingredients:

- 1 cup dried lentils (green or brown)
- 1 onion, diced
- 2 carrots, diced
- 2 celery stalks, diced
- 2 garlic cloves, minced
- 2 tablespoons olive oil
- 4 cups vegetable or chicken broth
- 2 bay leaves
- 1 teaspoon dried thyme
- Salt and pepper, to taste
- Chopped fresh parsley, for garnish

Instructions:

1. Prepare Lentils: Rinse the dried lentils under cold water. Set aside.
2. Sauté Vegetables: In a large pot or Dutch oven, heat olive oil over medium heat. Add diced onion, carrots, celery, and minced garlic. Sauté until vegetables start to soften, about 5-7 minutes.
3. Cook Lentils: Add the rinsed lentils to the pot along with the vegetable or chicken broth. Stir in bay leaves and dried thyme. Bring to a boil, then reduce heat to low and simmer uncovered for about 20-25 minutes, or until lentils are tender.
4. Season and Serve: Remove bay leaves from the stew. Season with salt and pepper to taste. Ladle into bowls and garnish with chopped fresh parsley.

Tips for Enjoying Lenticulae:

- Variety of Lentils: Experiment with different types of lentils, such as green, brown, or red lentils, depending on availability and desired texture.
- Enhance Flavor: Use a combination of herbs, spices, and aromatics to enhance the flavor of lentil dishes.
- Customize to Taste: Feel free to add extra vegetables, meat, or seafood to lentil dishes based on personal preferences and dietary needs.

By exploring the versatility of lentils and embracing ancient Roman culinary influences, you can create delicious and nutritious lenticulae-inspired dishes that celebrate the rich heritage of Roman gastronomy. Customize the recipes to suit your taste and enjoy the timeless appeal of lentils in Roman-style preparations!

Isicium de Lepore: Rabbit or hare dishes prepared with spices.

Ingredients:

- 1 rabbit or hare, cleaned and cut into serving pieces
- 2-3 tablespoons olive oil
- 1 onion, finely chopped
- 2-3 garlic cloves, minced
- 1 teaspoon ground black pepper
- 1 teaspoon ground cumin
- 1 teaspoon ground coriander
- 1/2 teaspoon ground cinnamon
- Salt, to taste
- 1 cup chicken or vegetable broth
- Fresh parsley, chopped (for garnish)

Instructions:

1. Prepare the Rabbit or Hare: Rinse the rabbit or hare under cold water and pat dry with paper towels. Cut into serving pieces, such as legs, loins, and shoulders.
2. Sauté the Aromatics: In a large skillet or Dutch oven, heat olive oil over medium heat. Add chopped onion and minced garlic. Sauté until the onions are translucent and aromatic.
3. Season the Meat: Season the rabbit or hare pieces with ground black pepper, cumin, coriander, cinnamon, and salt. Rub the spices into the meat evenly.
4. Brown the Meat: Increase the heat to medium-high. Add the seasoned rabbit or hare pieces to the skillet, and brown on all sides for a few minutes.
5. Add Broth and Simmer: Pour in the chicken or vegetable broth to the skillet. Bring to a simmer, then reduce the heat to low. Cover and cook for about 45-60 minutes, or until the rabbit or hare is tender and cooked through. Check the meat periodically and add more broth if needed.
6. Adjust Seasoning: Taste and adjust the seasoning with salt and pepper if necessary.
7. Serve: Transfer the cooked Isicium de Lepore to a serving platter. Garnish with chopped fresh parsley.

Tips for Enjoying Isicium de Lepore:

- Herb Variations: Experiment with other Roman herbs such as lovage, rue, or mint for a more authentic flavor.

- Accompaniments: Serve Isicium de Lepore with Roman-style bread (panis), olives, or a simple salad dressed with vinegar and olive oil.
- Wine Pairing: Pair this dish with a Roman-style wine or a dry red wine for a complementary dining experience.

By embracing the flavors of ancient Rome and preparing Isicium de Lepore with traditional spices and techniques, you can enjoy a taste of history and appreciate the culinary heritage of rabbit and hare dishes in Roman cuisine. Customize the recipe to suit your preferences and immerse yourself in the timeless appeal of ancient Roman gastronomy!

Cochleae: Snails cooked with various seasonings.

Ingredients:

- 1 pound fresh or canned edible snails (escargot)
- 4 tablespoons olive oil
- 4 garlic cloves, minced
- 2 tablespoons fresh parsley, chopped
- 1 tablespoon fresh mint, chopped
- 1 tablespoon fresh rue (or substitute with oregano or thyme)
- Salt and pepper, to taste
- Red wine vinegar, for finishing (optional)

Instructions:

1. Prepare the Snails: If using fresh snails, clean and purge them according to the instructions provided with your snails. If using canned snails, drain and rinse them thoroughly.
2. Sauté the Aromatics: In a large skillet or frying pan, heat olive oil over medium heat. Add minced garlic and sauté until fragrant, about 1 minute.
3. Cook the Snails: Add the prepared snails to the skillet. Stir and cook for about 5-7 minutes, allowing the snails to heat through and absorb the flavors.
4. Add Herbs and Seasonings: Stir in chopped parsley, mint, and rue (or substitute herbs). Season with salt and pepper to taste. Continue to cook for another 2-3 minutes, stirring occasionally.
5. Finish with Vinegar (Optional): For added flavor, drizzle a small amount of red wine vinegar over the snails just before serving. This will enhance the tanginess of the dish.
6. Serve: Transfer the cooked cochleae to a serving dish. Garnish with additional chopped herbs if desired.

Tips for Enjoying Cochleae:

- Herb Variations: Experiment with different herbs and spices used in ancient Roman cuisine, such as lovage, dill, or coriander seeds.
- Accompaniments: Serve cochleae with crusty bread (panis) to soak up the flavorful juices or alongside a simple salad dressed with olive oil and vinegar.
- Wine Pairing: Pair this dish with a Roman-style wine or a crisp white wine to complement the savory flavors of the cochleae.

By recreating cochleae with traditional Roman seasonings and techniques, you can experience a taste of ancient Roman gastronomy and appreciate the culinary heritage of snail dishes in Roman cuisine. Adjust the recipe to suit your preferences and enjoy the unique flavors of cochleae prepared in the style of ancient Rome!

Gustum de Pomis: Apple-based dishes and desserts.

Ingredients:

- 4-5 apples, peeled, cored, and sliced
- 2 tablespoons honey
- 1/2 teaspoon ground cinnamon
- 1/4 teaspoon ground nutmeg
- 1/4 cup chopped walnuts or almonds
- Pinch of salt
- Olive oil or melted butter, for greasing
- Optional: Red wine for poaching (substitute with water if desired)
- Fresh mint leaves, for garnish

Instructions:

1. Prepare the Apples: Peel, core, and slice the apples into wedges or chunks.
2. Poach the Apples (Optional): In a saucepan, combine the apple slices with enough red wine (or water) to cover them. Bring to a gentle simmer and poach the apples until they are tender, about 5-7 minutes. Remove from heat and drain excess liquid.
3. Combine Ingredients: In a bowl, toss the poached (or raw) apple slices with honey, ground cinnamon, ground nutmeg, chopped nuts, and a pinch of salt. Ensure the apples are well coated with the mixture.
4. Grease Baking Dish: Preheat the oven to 350°F (175°C). Grease a baking dish or oven-proof skillet with olive oil or melted butter.
5. Arrange Apple Mixture: Spread the coated apple slices evenly in the greased baking dish.
6. Bake: Place the baking dish in the preheated oven and bake for 20-25 minutes, or until the apples are tender and caramelized around the edges.
7. Serve: Remove the Gustum de Pomis from the oven. Let it cool slightly before serving. Garnish with fresh mint leaves for a pop of color and extra freshness.

Tips for Enjoying Gustum de Pomis:

- Variations: Experiment with different apple varieties such as sweet or tart apples to vary the flavor and sweetness of the dish.
- Serve with Accompaniments: Enjoy Gustum de Pomis on its own as a simple dessert, or pair it with a dollop of whipped cream, Greek yogurt, or a scoop of vanilla ice cream for added indulgence.

- Incorporate Roman Flavors: Enhance the dish with Roman-inspired spices like cloves, cardamom, or black pepper for a unique twist.

By preparing Gustum de Pomis with traditional Roman ingredients and flavors, you can experience a taste of ancient Roman cuisine and enjoy the delightful combination of apples, honey, and spices in a classic dessert. Customize the recipe to suit your preferences and savor the rich heritage of apple-based dishes in Roman gastronomy!

www.ingramcontent.com/pod-product-compliance
Lightning Source LLC
LaVergne TN
LVHW081607060526
838201LV00054B/2117